—— DISTINGUISHED STUDIES IN ——

American Legal and Constitutional History

Harold M. Hyman, General Editor
William P. Hobby Professor of History
Rice University

A Garland Series

REVOLUTION TO THE RIGHT

Criminal Procedure Jurisprudence
during the Burger-Rehnquist
Court Era

by
John F. Decker

Garland Publishing, Inc.
New York & London   1992

Library of Congress Cataloging-in-Publication Data

Decker, John F., 1944–
    Revolution to the right : criminal procedure jurisprudence during
the Burger-Rehnquist court era / by John F. Decker.
        p.   cm. — (Distinguished studies in American legal and
constitutional history)
    Includes index.
    ISBN 0-8153-1250-4; ISBN 0-8153-1541-4 (pbk.)
    1. Criminal procedure—United States—History. 2. Civil rights—
United States—History. 3. Due process of law—United States—
History. 4. United States. Supreme Court—History. I. Title.
II. Series.
KF9619.D43   1992
345.73'-05—dc20   92-44251
[347.3055]   CIP

All volumes are printed on acid-free, 250-year-life paper
Manufactured in the United States of America

Designed by Kathryn Semble

Contents

Preface

SOCIAL CONDITIONS and historical events prompted the United States Supreme Court, during the tenure of Chief Justice Earl Warren, to insure that the civil rights of various minority groups be protected in various contexts. During this period between 1953 and 1968, the Court was determined, for example, to provide racial minorities with equal access to education, guarantee women fair opportunities in the workplace, and protect political minorities' right to speech and assembly. Although many of the Warren Court decisions that expanded civil liberties proved controversial, none were more so than those cases wherein the court dramatically enlarged the rights of persons accused of crime.

In rapid fire succession, the Warren Court issued opinion after opinion that in one way or another increased suspects' rights to be free of unreasonable searches and seizures, avoid self-incrimination and double jeopardy, and benefit from various trial guarantees, including assistance of counsel and confrontation of the accuser. The net effect of these judicial developments was to move the criminal justice system from an institution that emphasized law enforcement objectives as the paramount, if not sole, goal to one where due process and presumption of innocence concerns were viewed as equally important to the conviction of the guilty.

Following the (1) 1968 presidential election, where Richard Nixon and George Wallace made the United States Supreme Court's "activism" a major political issue and (2) the resignation of Chief Justice Warren as well as several other justices, now President Nixon appointed four new justices, including Chief Justice Warren Burger, to the court during his first presidential term.

These new justices were promoted as adherents to a "judicial conservatism" that would discontinue the "revolutionary" and, to many, unsettling change in the constitutional landscape. In point of fact, the Burger Court and, more recently, the Rehnquist Court have not only managed to reverse the trend of expanding the rights of the accused, but they have also dramatically undercut the Warren Court decisions to such an extent that the "criminal justice" system has now returned to a law enforcement tool where due process and fairness concerns are significantly minimized.

Moreover, the "judicial conservatism" badge placed on the post-Warren Court has actually been used as a veil to mask the Court's continued *activism*. All that has changed is the Court's direction, certainly not its speed. I wrote *Revolution to the Right* not only to chronicle these developments during and after the Warren Court period, but also to detail how the Court has profoundly changed constitutional criminal procedure in an attempt to serve a conservative political agenda and the law enforcement establishment. Also, I question whether the diminution of the rights of suspects has actually paid dividends in the quest for crime control. Finally, I believe it important to advance the thesis that this diminishing of the rights of all accused portends a serious threat to the human rights of all citizens in the United States.

John F. Decker
Professor of Law
DePaul University
Chicago, Illinois
October 1992

Acknowledgments

THE AUTHOR expresses sincere gratitude to Dean John Roberts and the staff of the DePaul University College of Law for their support throughout this endeavor. In addition, I wish to thank my family and friends for their support, tolerance, and understanding as this work progressed.

I wish to express special thanks to Ziad Alnaqib, David Brickey and John Roberts for their review of this work. Further, I wish to acknowledge the outstanding support of Joseph Borsberry, Matthew Gloss, Annette Toliver and Janet Vander Kelen in the production and editing of the manuscript.

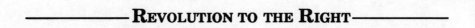
REVOLUTION TO THE RIGHT

CHAPTER 1

Symbolism: An Introduction

THERE ARE few persons who have studied the evolution of American criminal procedure over the last thirty years who would quibble with the proposition that the Supreme Court, during what might be described as the Warren Court Era, went to considerable lengths to broaden the procedural rights of persons charged with criminal offenses.[1] Possibly as a by-product of a new sensitivity about basic freedoms that developed during the civil rights era of the 1950s and the 1960s,[2] the Court ruled in a host of 1960s decisions that virtually all of the protections contained within the Bill of Rights were part and parcel of the Fourteenth Amendment due process protections and, thus, were imposed on the various states.[3]

The Warren Court's efforts seemed to fall into four categories in terms of the purposes it attempted to achieve in its rulings.[4] First, there were those decisions that sought to eliminate the invidious effects of poverty on an individual's ability to exercise her or his fundamental rights when facing the criminal justice system.[5] For example, the decision of *Gideon v. Wainwright*,[6] which provided that indigent defendants had a right to appointed counsel at trial, was designed to put a defendant with little or no financial resources on roughly equal footing with (1) a defendant who could afford to hire a defense attorney and, in addition, (2) the state that had the resources to hire a lawyer to handle the prosecution of the defendant at trial.

Second, there were those rulings that had as their purpose the safeguarding and effectuating of already recognized rights.[7] To illustrate, although the Supreme Court had already ruled the Fourth Amendment prohibition against unreasonable searches and seizures was a fundamental right at the state level,[8] the Court felt compelled, in *Mapp v. Ohio*,[9] to hold the exclusionary bar against the government's use of unconstitutionally seized evidence[10] was essential in a state trial court in order to deter state police from running roughshod over its citizens' Fourth Amendment guarantees.[11]

A third group of cases were designed to reconsider existing rights in the face of new challenges to those rights.[12] Here, again, it is

3

appropriate to consider an example. It is certainly doubtful that the
Framers of the Bill of Rights gave any thought to the prospect of the
government's use of electronic surveillance of conversations as they
might attempt to build a case against a criminal suspect and, also
how such governmental action might intrude on the suspect's
constitutional liberties. The early decisions addressing this subject,[13]
and, for that matter, other types of government evidence-gathering
methods, focused the Fourth Amendment inquiry on a "trespass" or
property-oriented analysis.[14] In the electronic monitoring context, where
the electronic eavesdropping of a suspect's conversation did not involve
a physical trespass by government agents upon the suspect's property,
such as where the authorities installed a wiretap on the suspect's
telephone line from a point outside his premises[15] or used a
detectaphone placed against an office wall in order to hear a suspect's
conversation in his office next door,[16] there was no search or seizure
within the contemplation of the Fourth Amendment.[17] On the other
hand, if the electronic eavesdropping had been accomplished through
some act of "trespass" upon the suspect's private premises, then the
suspect's Fourth Amendment guarantees would have to be respected.[18]

Ultimately, the Warren Court concluded that this "trespass/no
trespass" approach to evaluating Fourth Amendment claims made
little sense in the landmark decision of *Katz v. United States*.[19] In
that case, the defendant had been using a public telephone booth to
advance his illegal gambling endeavors.[20] The government, in turn,
attached a hidden electronic listening device outside of the telephone
booth in question without judicial authorization.[21] Predictably, the
arguments of the respective parties ultimately heard by the court in
Katz focused on whether the booth was a "constitutionally protected
area."[22] However, the Court dramatically shifted the nature of the
constitutional inquiry when it stated "the Fourth Amendment protects
people" and their reasonable expectations of privacy, not mere
"places."[23] Here, they held Katz had a reasonable expectation of privacy
from the "uninvited ear" of the government as he spoke on the public
phone.[24] Any government intrusion upon that zone of privacy that
surrounded Katz had to be legitimated by a judicial order permitting
the electronic eavesdropping.[25] Thus, in one bold stroke, the Court
shifted Fourth Amendment jurisprudence from an evaluation of
property rights to a privacy analysis. The right of a *person* "to be let
alone"[26] from casual governmental scrutiny was now elevated to a
meaningful fundamental right.

The final category of cases expanding suspects' rights during the
tenure of Chief Justice Earl Warren were those wherein the Court
sought to provide roughly equal constitutional safeguards to those
accused persons who stood in state rather than federal court.[27] Here,

one must consider the myriad of cases in which the nation's high court incorporated into the due process guarantee the various protections contained in the Bill of Rights—those Fourth, Fifth, Sixth, and Eighth amendment rights afforded criminal defendants[28] that were previously reserved for defendants facing federal prosecutions. No longer were such protections as the right to counsel, a jury trial, or freedom from double jeopardy the sole province of those who found themselves in federal court rather than state court.

One would be remiss to conclude these various expansions of constitutional protections were beneficial only to those engaged with crime. Conversely, these protections through stricter police procedures can be argued to have elevated the credibility and integrity of law enforcement officers both in the streets and in the courts. As such, the integrity of the whole system is preserved and elevated. As Chief Justice Earl Warren observed in his book, *A Republic, If You Can Keep It,*

> [A] nation which enforces its laws while violating the fundamental rights of its citizens is contributing to its own destruction. We must have vigorous enforcement of the law, but that enforcement must be fair, equal in its application, and in accordance with our time-honored and loudly professed freedoms.[29]

Warren recognized that when the government ignores or violates the basic constitutional liberties of its citizens the needed fabric of a civilized community is likely undermined. This theme was hardly a new one. For instance, in 1928 Justice Louis Brandeis warned:

> In a government of laws, existence of the government will be imperiled if it fails to observe the law scrupulously. Our government is the potent, the omnipresent teacher.... [I]t teaches the whole people by its example. Crime is contagious. If the government becomes a lawbreaker, it breeds contempt for law; invites every man to become a law unto himself; it invites anarchy.[30]

Brandeis recognized that a greater respect for the Bill of Rights protections guaranteed criminal suspects might impede to some extent efficiency in law enforcement objectives.[31] But such was the price a society would have to pay in order to preserve its basic freedoms. As Justice Oliver Wendell Holmes, who concurred with Brandeis' observation, put it: "We have to choose, and for my part I think it a lesser evil that some criminals should escape than that the government should play an ignoble part."[32] In any event, the Warren Court was committed to the proposition that due process demanded an array of procedural protections in the criminal justice system that were truly meaningful and substantive. Toward the end of the Warren

Court Era, Professor Herbert Packer pointed out in his book entitled, *The Limits of the Criminal Sanction*, that there are in essence two different models of criminal justice: (1) a "due process model," which places primary emphasis on fairness, equity and civility toward an accused as well as the doctrine of innocence until proven guilty; and (2) a "crime control model," which places a premium on efficiency in apprehension and conviction, finality of result and a presumption of guilt.[33] Packer observed that the Warren Court in its decisions involving criminal procedure had clearly embarked on a journey away from the crime control model and toward the due process approach.[34]

Predictably, the due process focus of the Warren Court rulings in the criminal procedure context was the target of considerable criticism.[35] Indeed, Richard Nixon and George Wallace made these Warren Court rulings an issue in the 1968 presidential election when they called upon voters to elect "law and order."[36] Having been accused of "coddling criminals,"[37] the Warren Court was called upon by President Nixon to "reverse the trend toward crime and violence, to reinstill a respect for law in all our people."[38] Nixon made four new appointments to the Court during his first term—Burger, Blackmun, Powell, and Rehnquist. These new justices, along with those justices already on the Court who had previously dissented against the Warren majority's dramatic changes in criminal procedure jurisprudence, were prepared to heed the cries for "law and order" and shift the Court to positions more akin to "crime control" objectives.[39]

As the pulling and tugging between the "due process model" and the "crime control model" of the criminal justice system continued during the Burger Court Era,[40] the court placed a greater emphasis on the ultimate question of whether the accused was actually guilty of the offense.[41] Result was now taking precedent over process. Clearly, this newly constituted court and the Rehnquist Court that followed did *not*, as it had the power to do so, completely dismantle the Warren Court protections. Rather, a pattern of decision making surfaced that either (1) halted the further development of procedural guarantees that might have otherwise followed the original line of the Warren Court rulings or (2) gradually and subtly unraveled the fundamental bases of these decisions. Here, the Burger and Rehnquist Courts, respectively, were not about to overrule cavalierly Warren Court precedent while totally ignoring the concept of *stare decisis*, thereby opening themselves up to many of the criticisms earlier directed at the Warren Court. These latter courts could not instantly reform the arrangement that they had inherited lest they be accused of "judicial activism" at a time when judicial conservatism was in vogue. More importantly, they could not dramatically shift their direction toward positions of the government in the criminal justice arena, otherwise they might come to be viewed as guardians of the police rather than the guardians of the people. While the Warren Court was accused of ignoring *stare decisis*, the subsequent Burger and Rehnquist Courts gracefully slalomed and nicked the new precedents of the Warren Court.

These were not times for bold moves; it was time for delicate maneuvering. The need for the appearance of stability outweighed the need to heed the cries of critics of the Warren Court who called for an immediate return to the "good old days" of expeditious and tough law enforcement. Thus, a more calm, cautious, and calculated jurisprudence to judicial decision making of criminal procedure disputes replaced the almost rapid-fire[42] and revolutionary[43] change that preceded it in the Warren Court Era. Now, the Court would focus on a distinction, sometimes artificial, between the case at hand and the earlier pro-defendant decision.[44] In other disputes where doctrinal conflict had always been inherent in the resolution of the case, the Court might deemphasize the importance of the theory that usually won out in yesteryear and place greater emphasis on the contrary theory in order to achieve a different outcome, one that was more palatable to law enforcement endeavors.[45] In still others, the Court would simply expand[46] or, if such was unavoidable, create a new exception[47] to the Warren Court rule. Or, it would rediscover a concept that may have previously lost most of its utility and reuse it in the immediate case to thwart effectively the impact of the Warren Court view of the concept.[48]

Notwithstanding the subtlety inherent in this judicial scheme, the Burger and Rehnquist courts have managed to erode, if not outright reverse, the due process guarantees of Warren Court holdings. The "due process" approach embraced by the Warren Court has been replaced by what may be described as *symbolic* gestures that reflect only an *appearance* of meaningful due process but which, upon close examination, turns out to be a true "crime control model" in operation. For instance, imposing the exclusionary rule on the states during the Warren Court period was purportedly designed to discourage governmental non-compliance with the constitutional rights of its citizens. However, a review of the most recent exclusionary rule cases, which will be undertaken later in this volume,[49] including the various exceptions and doctrinal limitations on the reach of the rule, reveals a rule that may now only marginally deter unconstitutional police mischief in evidence gathering. On the other hand, it will be seen that the Court still retains the rule in some form since the general rule advances a *perception* of discontent with the police running roughshod over the personal liberties of members of the American community.

The Fourth Amendment barrier against unreasonable searches and seizures was presumably developed by the Framers of the Bill of Rights to guard basic freedoms in the face of possible overzealous police scrutiny of individuals within our democratic society. The Warren Court steadfastly injected in their constitutional interpretation of this important right doctrinal elements designed to make this right a truly *meaningful* one. Thus, for example, the *Katz* doctrine, which clarified that the Fourth Amendment was designed to protect the *privacy* of people, not their "mere places," reflected a significant advance in Fourth Amendment civil libertarian jurisprudence. However, the post-Warren Court's use of the "public exposure" doctrine as well as the "reasonableness" standard, which will be explored below,[50] have whittled away Fourth Amendment protections to such an extent that they may now be viewed as largely illusory.

The same might be said about the Fifth Amendment privilege against self-incrimination in the context of police interrogation. The so-called *Miranda* warning, originally designed by the Warren Court to assure police suspects have a full understanding of their rights during interrogation, provides less assurance now because various Burger and Rehnquist court decisions seem to rely on every possible escape device to avoid application of these admonishments. These Burger and Rehnquist court decisions will also be examined in this study.[51]

The right to counsel guaranteed by the Sixth Amendment was dramatically expanded by a series of post-*Gideon* decisions that were issued by the United States Supreme Court during the Warren Era. More recent case law has, however, brought an abrupt halt to the pattern of expansion reflected in earlier opinions. These cases will also be studied in due course in this book.[52]

A more thorough review of these aforementioned concerns—the exclusionary rule, the Fourth Amendment barrier against unreasonable searches and seizures, the Fifth Amendment privilege and related *Miranda* issues, and the Sixth Amendment right to appointed counsel—which will be the primary focus of this work—will reveal a distinct change in emphasis between the Warren Court decisions and the later Burger and Rehnquist rulings. Close scrutiny of the evolution of these concerns reveals the nation's highest court has consciously or unconsciously become content with giving only lip service to fundamental constitutional guarantees while simultaneously responding to law enforcement arguments that vigorous enforcement of the Bill of Rights will interfere with effective crime control. General *pronouncements* regarding their recognition of civil rights have replaced steadfast *application* of these rights. More often than in the past, today's libertarian pronouncements that appear in the opinions of the

United States Supreme Court are mere dictum. More often, application of these rights gives way to the law enforcement imperatives of affirming the conviction. More often, the Court's case law pontifications about the Bill of Rights are symbolic exercises—an effort to placate the citizenry that our nation is not a police state. More often, substantive mandates that flowed from the Court's interpretations of the Bill of Rights in yesteryear are replaced with case law rhetoric designed to pacify those who continue to insist on a freedom from police excess.

Realizing that the rights of criminal suspects and certain police initiatives do not live comfortably side by side, a substitute arrangement had to be designed. The inherent conflict in affording criminal suspects with meaningful procedural protections and providing the larger community with security from the criminal element had to somehow be avoided in the Court's resolution of criminal procedure cases and controversies. Societal calls for a "war on crime" made the thought of imposing marked adjustments on the actions of the law enforcement establishment a practical impossibility. Effective police endeavors could not be sacrificed on the altar of the Bill of Rights. Thus, a new scheme of decision making now appears in the arena of criminal procedure.

The shape of today's opinions looks something like the following: First, rather than belittle the Constitution, sing loud praises about the Bill of Rights. Make *sounds* like those that are expected from a body that has been delegated the responsibility for *defending* the Bill of Rights. Quote in full the text of the constitutional provision at issue. Recite the litany of *earlier* decisions that relate to the issue at hand wherein the Court granted the defendant-petitioner's claim for relief. Remind the reader of the opinion that the Court has previously injected some form of due process protection into the procedural setting under discussion. Suggest, where possible, that there is already plenty of due process protections surrounding the proceeding at issue. Next, focus on the ugly nature of the defendant's crime. Then, clinically review the procedural steps *this* defendant has already experienced—that following his arrest, he confessed, was positively identified by witnesses or a victim, was indicted by a grand jury of citizens, was convicted by a jury of his peers at trial, had his conviction affirmed by the appellate court and, later, by the state supreme court. Paint a picture of a defendant who had his day in court, maybe too many days. Paint a picture of a law enforcement and judicial system that methodically, carefully, and fairly established an air-tight case against the defendant. Finally, focus on the narrow issue at hand. Draw a distinction from the prior case. Develop an exception to the prior rule. If error is found, find it to be harmless error. Deny relief. Affirm the conviction.

The arguments supporting the possible merits of the petitioner's claim for procedural due process are now often drowned out by symbols of fairness and justice. The constitutional provision was examined. Precedent was scrutinized. The petitioner's claim for relief was examined. The symbol of *fairness* rings loud. Defendant's misdeeds are documented. Layers of damning evidence are reviewed. The prosecutorial and judicial inquiry pointing to the defendant's guilt are noted. The symbol of *justice* rings loud.

In his autumn years, Justice William O. Douglas made the following remarks as he complained in his autobiography about Chief Justice Burger's efforts to reduce the "workload" of the United States Supreme Court:[53]

> What was happening, I think, was that Nixon and his followers wanted *law and order*. What the Hughes, Stone and Warren Court had been giving the country was *constitutional law and order*. The Establishment did not like it . . . .
>
> The Richard Nixon-George Wallace philosophy of irritating those raw spots activated forces that prevented the healing of past conflicts. *Constitutional law and order* was shouted down. *Constitutional law and order* was discarded . . . . The Supreme Court, an important symbol of the Constitution, was shoved more and more into the background. Cutting down its "workload" . . . would keep it alive as a symbol but it would no longer be able to vindicate rights of the oppressed. It would keep the solemn, benign face of the Establishment, letting the country know that "law and order" was in control and that the Constitution—so far as human rights were concerned—was kept on ice.[54]

NOTES

1. Charles Whitebread & Christopher Slobogin, CRIMINAL PROCEDURE: AN ANALYSIS OF CASES AND CONCEPTS 1–3 (2nd ed. 1986).

2. *See id.* at 1.

3. *Id.* at 2–3, citing to (1) the Fourth Amendment exclusionary rule remedy, Mapp v. Ohio, 367 U.S. 643 (1961); (2) the Fifth Amendment privilege against self-incrimination, Malloy v. Hogan, 378 U.S. 1 (1964); prohibition against double jeopardy, Benton v. Maryland, 395 U.S. 784 (1969) and the reasonable doubt standard in criminal trials, *In re* Winship, 397 U.S. 358 (1970); (3) the Sixth Amendment right to a speedy trial, Klopfer v. North Carolina, 386 U.S.

213 (1967), a jury trial, Duncan v. Louisiana, 391 U.S. 145 (1968), appointed counsel, Gideon v. Wainwright, 372 U.S. 335 (1963), confront one's accuser's, Pointer v. Texas, 380 U.S. 400 (1965), and compulsory process, Washington v. Texas, 388 U.S. 14 (1967); and, (4) the Eighth Amendment ban on cruel and unusual punishment, Robinson v. California, 370 U.S. 660 (1962).

4. Arthur Goldberg, EQUAL JUSTICE: THE WARREN ERA OF THE SUPREME COURT, 9 (1971).

5. *Id.* at 9–11.

6. 372 U.S. 335 (1963).

7. Goldberg, *supra* note 4, at 11–14.

8. Wolf v. Colorado, 338 U.S. 25 (1949).

9. 367 U.S. 643 (1963).

10. This rule first appeared in a case involving a federal agency's violation of a defendant's rights. *See* Weeks v. United States, 232 U.S. 383 (1914).

11. 367 U.S. at 657–659.

12. Goldberg, *supra* note 4, at 14–18.

13. *See, e.g.,* Olmstead v. United States, 277 U.S. 438 (1928).

14. *Id.* at 463–66. In addition, the *Olmstead* Court stated that Fourth Amendment protections would be implicated if the subject of the search and seizure involved some tangible object that, of course, is not present in an electronic eavesdropping situation. *Id. See* John Decker & Joel Handler, *Electronic Eavesdropping Standards, Restrictions and Remedies,* 12 CAL. W. L. REV. 60 (1975) for a discussion of developments in this area.

15. Olmstead v. United States, 277 U.S. 438 (1928).

16. Goldstein v. United States, 316 U.S. 114 (1942).

17. Notes 15–16 *supra.*

18. Silverman v. United States, 365 U.S. 505 (1961) (use of "spike mike" that intruded into defendant's premises held unconstitutional).

19. 389 U.S. 347, 350–53 (1967).

20. *Id.* at 348.

21. *Id.*

22. *Id.* at 349–351.

23. *Id.* at 351, 353.

24. *Id.* at 353.

25. *Id.* at 354–359.

26. Olmstead v. United States, 277 U.S. 438, 471–72 (1928) (Brandeis, J., dissenting).

27. Goldberg, *supra* note 4, at 18–20.

28. *See* note 3 *supra.*

29. Earl Warren, A REPUBLIC, IF YOU CAN KEEP IT, 102 (1972).

30. Olmstead v. United States, 277 U.S. 438, 473–74 (1928) (Brandeis, J., dissenting).

31. *Id.*

32. *Id.* at 471, (Holmes, J., dissenting) (discussing the need for application of the exclusionary rule).

33. Herbert Packer, THE LIMITS OF THE CRIMINAL SANCTION, 149–73 (1968).

34. *Id.* at 239–46.

35. *See, e.g.*, Robert Burns, *Due Process of Law: After 1890 Anything; Today Everything, A Bicentennial Proposal to Restore its Original Meaning*, 35 DEPAUL L. REV. 773 (1986); Fred Inbau, *Over-Reaction: The Mischief of Miranda v. Arizona*, 18 THE PROSECUTOR 7 (Winter 1985); Fred Inbau & James P. Manak, *Miranda v. Arizona—Is It Worth the Cost?*, 21 THE PROSECUTOR 31 (Spring 1988); Fred Inbau, *Law Enforcement, the Courts and Individual Civil Liberties*, CRIMINAL JUSTICE IN OUR TIME, 97 (A. Howard ed. 1965).

36. Theodore White, THE MAKING OF A PRESIDENT: 1968, 188–189 (1969).

37. George F. Cole, POLITICS AND THE ADMINISTRATION OF JUSTICE, 221–27 (1973), *citing* Fred P. Graham, THE SELF INFLICTED WOUND 288, 330 (1970).

38. Louis M. Kohlmeier, Jr., GOD SAVE THIS HONORABLE COURT 200 (1972).

39. Whitebread & Slobogin, *supra* note 1, at 3–4.

40. The use of the terms "Warren Court," "Burger Court," and "Rehnquist Court" as used herein are not designed to suggest a certain block of justices in the majority always adhered to the same point of view or always voted together. It is merely a shorthand way of describing a pattern of court decisions that—during the tenure of Chief Justice Warren—often sided with due process claimants and later—during the tenure of Chief Justice Burger and Chief Justice Rehnquist—more often sided with law enforcement arguments. *See* Whitebread & Slobogin, *supra* note 1, at 3–4, note 23 for a similar admonishment.

41. *See, e.g.*, United States v. Russell, 411 U.S. 423, 436 (1973) (in dismissing defendant's entrapment claim, it is important to note that the defendant was not an "unwary innocent," but an "unwary criminal"); Ross v. Moffit, 417 U.S. 600, 610–11 (1974) (defendant not entitled to appointed counsel in a discretionary appeal since defendant would be using such counsel "as a sword to upset the prior determination of guilt"); United States v. Lovasco, 431 U.S. 783, 790–96 (1983) (where the prosecution does not seek an indictment immediately after the defendant's commission of a crime and instead delays such prosecution until a later juncture that he deems more appropriate to "establish [defendant's] guilt beyond a reasonable doubt," there is no denial of the defendant's right to due process "even if his defense might have been somewhat prejudiced by the lapse of time" between the commission of the crime and its prosecution); United v. Scott, 437 U.S. 82, 87–101 (1978) (where defendant successfully moved to dismiss his indictment following the presentation of all evidence at trial but before the case was submitted to the jury, double jeopardy does not bar a retrial since "defendant elected to seek termination of the trial on [procedural] grounds unrelated to guilt or innocence"); United States v. Havens, 446 U.S. 620, 624–28 (1980) (exclusionary rule does not bar at trial the use of illegally seized evidence for impeachment purposes, and to hold otherwise would result in the "impairment of the fact-finding goals of the criminal trial"); Strickland v. Washington, 466 U.S. 668, 691–96 (1984) (regarding incompetency of counsel claims and other procedural errors, the "question is whether there is a reasonable probability that, absent

the errors, the fact finder would have a reasonable doubt respecting guilt"); Kuhlman v. Wilson, 106 S.Ct. 2616, 2627 (1986) (while denying a state convict's petition for habeas corpus relief, it is important to note the "ends of justice" only "require federal courts to entertain such petitions ... where the prisoner supplements his constitutional claim with a colorable showing of factual innocence").

42. *See, e.g.*, Whitebread & Slobogin, *supra*, note 3.

43. *See* THE CRIMINAL LAW REVOLUTION AND ITS AFTERMATH: 1960–72 (Editors of Criminal Law Reporter 1973).

44. In the context of corporeal identifications—lineups and showups—the Court ruled in United States v. Wade, 388 U.S. 218 (1967), that a formally charged defendant had a right to appointed counsel guaranteed by the Sixth Amendment, which the Court stated was an essential guard against the potential of irreparable mistaken identifications by witnesses to a crime. However, in Kirby v. Illinois, 406 U.S. 682 (1972), the Court ruled that a defendant *not* formally charged had no similar right to appointed counsel. In *Kirby*, the Court rested its ruling heavily on the defendant not yet having been faced with a formal charge, unlike in *Wade* where the defendant had been already indicted. One must ask, however, if the Court's reliance on such a distinction made any sense? If the *Wade* pronouncement was based on concerns regarding erroneous identifications and the need to have attorney present to guard against such mistaken identification, what difference should it make whether the accused was formally charged or not? Moreover, *Kirby*, essentially eliminates the significance of *Wade* where police simply conduct a lineup before formal charge in order to avoid the rigors of *Wade*.

A second situation involving a claim for a right to appointed counsel could be used as an illustration. First, in Douglass v. California, 372 U.S. 353 (1963), the Court ruled a defendant had a right to appointed counsel at his first appeal, which he enjoys as a matter of right by reason of equal protection of law. However, in Ross v. Moffit, 417 U.S. 600 (1974), the Court ruled equal protection does not require appointed counsel in a defendant's second discretionary appeal before the state's highest court nor in his request for discretionary review by the United States Supreme Court. In *Ross*, the Court stated that unlike in a trial where a defendant needs appointed counsel to serve as a "shield" against an erroneous conviction, in the appellate arena he would be using his counsel as a "sword to upset the prior determination of guilt." *Id*. at 610–11. The Court concluded that defendant had a right to an attorney as a shield but not as a sword. If such is the case, however, than what principle supports the *Douglas* equal protection right where the defendant is also using his appointed counsel as a sword in his first appeal?

In addition, the *Ross* Court stated equal protection is designed "only to assure the indigent defendant an adequate opportunity to present his claims fairly in the context of the state's appellate process." *Id*. at 616. The Court felt that providing defendant appointed counsel on his first appeal but not doing so in his second, discretionary appeal was consistent with the aforesaid standard. But, again, what principle justifies such differential treatment? If a state determines a first appeal step should be followed by a second appeal step to assure the accuracy of appellate resolution of the issues in its appellate process, why should the indigent defendant be denied meaningful access to the second step?

45. Double jeopardy protections might be used as an illustration. In the earlier cases, the Court seemed to focus on the need to protect an accused from *repeated* prosecutions. For example, in Green v. United States, 355 U.S. 184 (1957), the Court stated:

> the underlying idea, one that is deeply ingrained in at least the Anglo-American system of jurisprudence, is that the state with all of its resources and power should not be allowed to make repeated attempts to convict an individual for an alleged offense, thereby subjecting him to embarrassment, expense and ordeal and compelling him to live in a continuing state of anxiety and insecurity, as well as enhancing the possibility that even though innocent, he may be found guilty.

Id. at 191–93. Following such reasoning, the Court ruled a retrial of an accused would be barred by double jeopardy even though a mid-trial dismissal of charges against the accused was not based "on the merits" of guilt or innocence. United States v. Jenkins, 430 U.S. 258 (1975).

Later, the Court deemphasized the repeated prosecutions theme and focused instead on whether the outcome of the earlier trial was "unrelated to factual guilt or innocence." United States v. Scott, 437 U.S. 82, 92–94 (1978). If the dismissal of the charges at the defendant's initial trial were not based on a factual finding of innocence, then a second trial would be permitted. *Id.* (where defendant successfully moved for dismissal of two counts of his indictment on grounds of prejudicial pretrial delay; retrial not barred by double jeopardy). If the dismissal of the charges was not based on some type of procedural error but instead the charges at the defendant's earlier trial had been set aside because the evidence against the accused was insufficient as a matter of law to prove his guilt, then a retrial on such charges would be impermissible. Burks v. United States, 437 U.S. 1 (1978); Green v. Masey, 437 U.S. 19 (1978); Hudson v. Louisiana, 450 U.S. 40 (1981).

46. In Chimel v. California, 395 U.S. 752 (1969), the Court narrowed the search incident to arrest exception to the Fourth Amendment warrant requirement to searches of "the arrestee's person and the area 'within his immediate control'—construing that phrase to mean the area from within which he might gain possession of a weapon or destructible evidence." *Id.* at 762–63. So long as the area in question was within the arrestee's "reach," the exception would apply. *Id.* at 765–66. In this case, evidence seized from various locations throughout the arrestee's residence was found to be outside the scope of the exception since they were clearly outside of his reach.

Later, in New York v. Belton, 453 U.S. 454 (1980), the Court expanded the exception in the automobile context when it held the passenger compartment and all containers in the passenger compartment could be searched under this exception even though the arrested occupants of the automobile were situated outside the automobile pursuant to a police order. *Id.* at 457–63. The Court held that since a passenger compartment is "generally, even if not inevitably," accessible to a "recent occupant" of an automobile, the search incident to arrest doctrine justified the police search and seizure of evidence in a jacket in the car. *Id.* at 462. The Court so ruled even though the New York Court of Appeals had determined the jacket was "inaccessible" to the defendants.

47. In Mapp v. Ohio, 367 U.S. 643 (1961), the Court ruled that evidence seized from a defendant in violation of his Fourth Amendment rights would be inadmissible as direct evidence of his guilt in a state trial court. However, in Massachusetts v. Shepard, 468 U.S. 981 (1984), the Court held evidence seized pursuant to a search warrant that violated the "particularity" requirement of the Fourth Amendment would be admissible under a so-called "good-faith" exception to the exclusionary rule since the officers executing the warrant believed that the defective warrant was a valid warrant.

48. The federal habeas corpus enactment provides a person convicted in state court must have "exhausted" available remedies in state court prior to petitioning a federal court for a writ of habeas corpus. 28 U.S.C. 2254. In Fay v. Noia, 372 U.S. 391 (1963), the Court ruled that a procedural default in state court, *i.e.*, a failure to avail oneself of previously available state remedy, would not bar a federal court from intervening and granting habeas corpus relief where a state claimant had pointed to a violation of federal constitutional rights *unless* it could be shown the petitioner had "deliberately bypassed the orderly procedure of the state court. . . ." *Id.* at 438.

If he "deliberately bypassed" his state remedies, the Court stated he would be found to have "forfeited his state remedies" and, accordingly, waived his right to federal habeas corpus review. *Id.* Since a "deliberate bypass" was difficult to demonstrate, state convicts petitioning a federal court for habeas corpus relief after *Fay* were considerably less likely to encounter a barrier to such relief on the grounds that they had waived available state remedies. *See generally* John H. Gibbons, *Waiver: Habeas Corpus Jurisdiction*, 2 SETON H.L.REV. 291 (1971).

In later cases, however, the Burger Court whittled away "deliberate bypass" standard and replaced it with the "cause and prejudice" standard for evaluating state arguments regarding petitioner waivers. *See* Francis v. Henderson, 425 U.S. 536 (1976); Wainwright v. Sykes, 433 U.S. 72 (1977). In Engle v. Isaac, 456 U.S. 107 (1982), it appeared the Court had clearly resurrected the waiver concept to bar federal court review of state convict petitions when it ruled "[a]ny prisoner bringing a constitutional claim to the federal courthouse after a state procedural default must demonstrate cause [for not raising the issue in a timely fashion in state court] and actual prejudice before obtaining relief." *Id.* at 129. *See* Jack A. Guttenberg, *Federal Habeas Corpus, Constitutional Rights and Procedural Forfeiture*, 12 HOFSTRA L.REV. 617 (1984).

49. *See* Chapter 2 *infra* and accompanying text.
50. *See* Chapter 3 *infra* and accompanying text.
51. *See* Chapter 4 *infra* and accompanying text.
52. *See* Chapter 5 *infra* and accompanying text.
53. *See* William Douglas, THE COURT YEARS, 378–92 (1980).
54. *Id.* at 391.

The Exclusionary Rule: The Constable Blundered, But So What?

IN 1914, in *Weeks v. United States*,[1] the United States Supreme Court ruled if evidence seized by federal agents in violation of a defendant's Fourth Amendment rights could be used against him at his trial on federal charges, the protection against unreasonable searches and seizures would be "of no value and, so far as those thus placed are concerned, might as well be stricken from the Constitution."[2] Thus the exclusionary rule was born. Later, in *Mapp v. Ohio*,[3] the Warren Court felt compelled to impose the rule in state court. The Court's reasons were twofold: (1) since other remedies, such as civil remedies, had proven to be "worthless and futile" in containing state police misconduct, the rule was necessary to deter state police from unreasonable searches and seizures "by removing the incentive to disregard" the Fourth Amendment;[4] and (2) to advance the "imperative of judicial integrity."[5]

> Nothing can destroy a government more quickly than its failure to observe its own laws, or worse, its disregard to the charter of its own existence.... Our government is the potent, the omnipresent teacher. For good or for ill, it teaches the whole people by its example.... If the government becomes a law-breaker, it breeds contempt for law; it invites every man to become a law unto himself; it invites anarchy.[6]

The roots of the due process model are evidenced in the above quote from Justice Brandeis; ours is a nation of laws, and the government must be subject to the principles of fair play that govern all of us. In a sense, then, the Fourth Amendment rulings of the Warren Court convey strong symbolic messages. The first message was directed at the police: do not be tempted, in your quest to establish or build a case against a law violator, to violate a higher law—a fundamental protection contained in the Bill of Rights. The second message was directed at the judiciary: courts of *law* must not handle muddy evidence lest their own hands be muddied.

Because of its dedication to communicate these messages in its Fourth Amendment jurisprudence, the Warren Court was accused of "coddling criminals" and labeled un-American. But, this was simply false and rhetorical. The Warren Court was convinced that what was worse than lawlessness and disorder was unconstitutional law and order, where the state is the illegal actor and its judicial branch its prime defender. Under such a system, the Court would indeed be coddling criminality—the criminality of the state.

However, the Burger and Rehnquist Courts, which elevated crime control objectives to the forefront of the criminal justice system, did not show the same respect for restraints on the state that the Warren Court thought imperative for a system based on due process. Both of these later Courts accepted the judiciary's handling of muddied evidence in various ways that the Warren Court would have rejected as violative of due process and would have considered to be at odds with our system of government accountability.

For example, notwithstanding a 1921 ruling that allowed several indicted defendants to challenge a grand jury's use of illegally seized evidence,[7] the United States Supreme Court in the 1974 case of *United States v. Calandra*[8] held the exclusionary rule should be "restricted to those areas where its remedial objectives are . . . most efficaciously served" and that the interests behind the exclusionary rule would *not* be advanced by excluding the use of illegal evidence in a grand jury inquiry.[9] Lower courts have interpreted this holding expansively and now allow the government to use affirmatively illegally seized evidence in *any criminal proceeding beyond trial*, such as sentencing hearings,[10] probation revocation hearings,[11] parole revocation hearings,[12] and supervision revocation hearings.[13]

Calandra and the various cases that follow its lead suffer several major flaws. These decisions focus almost exclusively on the exclusionary rule's deterrent purpose against police lawlessness and tend to ignore judicial integrity considerations and, in that regard, indicate the "remedy" should only be used where it will "significantly further" deterrence.[14] Steadfast adherence to a *principle* enforcing government compliance with the constitutional rule prohibiting illicit police action does not appear. In addition, even if it is legitimate to focus solely on deterrence, removal of the exclusionary rule from all criminal proceedings except the trial court itself can only *undermine* the deterrence of police misconduct.[15]

Similar to the Court's movement away from the invocation of the exclusionary rule in criminal proceeding beyond trial, the same pattern appears in connection with civil proceedings. In 1965, the Warren Court unanimously agreed in *One 1958 Plymouth Sedan v. Pennsylvania*[16] that the exclusionary rule applied in a state forfeiture proceeding.[17] Specifically, the Court held Pennsylvania's effort to gain a forfeiture of an automobile, because it had been used in the illegal transportation of liquor, could not be proved at the forfeiture hearing by the introduction into evidence of liquor taken from the car in an unconstitutional search.[18] Although forfeiture proceedings are technically civil inquiries, the Warren Court, nonetheless, indicated the inquiry was "quasi-criminal in character" because its object was "to penalize for the commission of an offense against the law."[19] Regardless of the nomenclature, this case represented an example of where the Warren Court was prepared to employ the exclusionary rule outside the criminal trial setting in its quest to advance the due process model of government.[20]

In 1976, the Burger Court decided *United States v. Janis,*[21] ruling the exclusionary rule had no application in a federal civil tax proceeding.[22] In *Janis*, after Los Angeles police obtained a warrant to search an alleged bookmaker's gambling paraphernalia, they seized wagering records and $4,940 in cash.[23] However, in a subsequent state criminal proceeding, the trial court ruled the evidence had been illegally seized since the affidavit supporting the warrant was faulty.[24] Meanwhile, the federal Internal Revenue Service had levied an assessment against Janis for his failure to file any federal tax returns in regards to his wagering income and sought to apply the $4,940 in cash against the total assessment.[25] Janis countered that since the gambling records and cash had been illegally seized, the records could not be used in the federal tax jeopardy proceeding to justify the tax assessment.[26] However, the *Janis* Court ultimately rejected this argument in a fashion quite similar to its approach in *Calandra.*[27]

Through its selective focus on police deterrence, deference to governmental conduct, and a lack of concern for judicial integrity, the Burger Court speculatively concluded, in the crime control tradition, that application of the exclusionary rule in Janis' case would only offer "marginal deterrence" and concluded the benefits of exclusion were outweighed by the "cost to society" of exclusion.[28] Furthermore, the *Janis* majority dismissed Justice Stewart's dissenting argument that the principle behind *One 1958 Plymouth Sedan* should govern this case as well since here, like the earlier case, "the civil proceeding serves as an adjunct to the enforcement of criminal law."[29]

Later, in *Immigration and Naturalization Service v. Lopez-Mendoza,*[30] the Burger Court refused to apply the exclusionary rule in a civil deportation proceeding, where the deportees were arrested illegally by I.N.S. agents.[31] Here, the cost-benefit analysis, now a regular feature of crime control Fourth Amendment analysis, was quite peculiar. For instance, on the "deterrent/benefit" side of the equation, the Court in *Lopez-Mendoza* stated that "[e]very I.N.S. agent knows . . . that it is highly unlikely that any particular arrestee will end up challenging the lawfulness of his arrest."[32] On the "cost" side, the Court noted that in deportation proceedings, "neither the hearing officers nor the attorneys. . . are likely to be well versed in the intricacies of Fourth Amendment law" and, accordingly, application of the law might complicate the proceeding.[33] Similarly ridiculous was the Court's point that since I.N.S. arrests often "occur in crowded or confused circumstances," utilization of the rule "might well result in the suppression of large amounts of information that had been obtained entirely lawfully."[34] Here, the Court's unusual calculus (1) effectively rewards governmental agents who "know" that their unconstitutional mischief will likely go unchallenged by the victims, (2) tolerates ignorance of constitutional law on the part of hearing officers and attorneys who handle immigration and deportation matters, (3) excuses police misconduct that stems from "crowded or confused circumstances," and (4) fails to recognize that if the "information" in question has "been obtained *entirely lawfully*," the exclusionary rule would *never be an issue* since the rule only arises where the police action is *unlawful*. Be that as it may, *Janis* and *Lopez-Mendoza* has been followed by lower courts' rejection of the exclusionary rule in many civil proceedings.[35]

Another example of the weakening of the exclusionary rule can be found in the Court's acceptance of the government's admission at the trial of illegally seized evidence for the purpose of impeaching a defendant's trial testimony.[36] In earlier cases, the Court had crafted a rule that a defendant's trial testimony could be impeached with illegally procured evidence but only where the tainted evidence was being used to contradict a *specific* statement made by the defendant during his *direct* examination.[37] In the 1925 decision of *Agnello v. United States*,[38] the Court forbade the government from using illegally seized cocaine to impeach the defendant's trial testimony because "[i]n his direct examination, Angelo was not asked and did not testify concerning the . . . cocaine."[39] Later, in *Walder v. United States*,[40] the Court allowed the government to impeach the defendant's trial testimony with tainted evidence in circumstances where the defendant on direct examination had made specific denials regarding having ever sold, possessed, or handled an illicit narcotic.[41] The Court was careful to qualify its holding:

> Of course, the Constitution guarantees a defendant the fullest opportunity to meet the accusation against him. He must be free to deny all the elements of the case against him without thereby giving leave to the government to introduce by way of rebuttal evidence illegally secured by it, and therefore not available for its case in chief.[42]

Here, the defendant had gone "beyond a mere denial of complicity" in the alleged criminality and instead had made a "sweeping claim" that he had never been involved in any type of illegal drug activity, which thereby allowed the government to impeach his statements with heroin that had been improperly seized from his premises.[43] Also, the Court noted this situation was different than *Agnello*, where the government "tried to smuggle it in on cross-examination . . . ."[44]

In the 1971 decision of *Harris v. New York*,[45] the Burger Court expanded the government's power to use illegally seized evidence to impeach a defendant's testimony when it ruled statements taken from an accused in violation of his rights under *Miranda v. Arizona*[46] could be used to attack the veracity of the defendant's trial testimony. By *Calandra*-type reasoning the Court justified this result, to wit, that extension of the exclusionary rule to this situation would have no appreciable effect in deterring police breaches of *Miranda*.[47] *Harris* was significant in that it (1) employed for the first time the impeachment exception to the exclusionary rule in a setting beyond a Fourth Amendment violation[48] and (2) deviated from dictum in *Miranda* that unambiguously stated the fruits of a *Miranda* violation could *not* be used by the government at trial for *any* purpose.[49] On the other hand, *Harris* did fall within the parameters of the *Agnello-Walder* limitation in that the government's impeachment effort was directed at defendant's *specific* denials made during his *direct* examination.[50]

By way of comparison, the *Harris* development was minuscule when considered against the 1980 decision *United States v. Havens*.[51] In that case, the defendant made general denials during his direct examination regarding involvement in the transportation of cocaine. During cross-examination the defendant denied for the first time that he had been involved in sewing a secret cloth pocket in his co-defendant's shirt, where drugs were eventually found, and having in his own suitcase another shirt from which a swatch of cloth had been cut to be used to make the secret pocket in question.[52] Thereafter, defendant's denials were rebutted by the admission of the shirt, which previously had been seized illegally from the defendant's suitcase.[53] After being instructed that they were to only consider the tainted evidence for the purpose of assessing the credibility of the defendant's denials, the jury convicted the defendant.[54] Subsequently, the United States Court of Appeals reversed the conviction on the grounds that the government's impeachment use of the illegally seized evidence exceeded the bounds of the *Agnello-Walder* exception. Here, the admission of the evidence was *not* in response to a *particular statement* made by the defendant during his *direct* examination.[55]

However, in a 5–4 decision, the United States Supreme Court reversed the federal appellate court ruling and held the earlier cases did *not* create "a flat rule permitting only statements on direct examination . . . ."[56] They ruled so long as a defendant's statements made during cross-examination "are plainly within the scope of the defendant's direct examination," these statements can be contradicted by illegally seized evidence.[57] The Court reasoned to allow false testimony during cross-examination to go unchallenged would impede the fact-finding goals of the criminal trial."[58]

The dissent in *Havens* did not mince words. It chastised the majority for not following precedent, particularly the *Agnello* barrier that precludes government's efforts to "smuggle" in the tainted evidence "on cross-examination."[59] Regarding the practical consequences of this ruling, the dissent pointed out:

> Criminal defendants now told that prosecutors are licensed to insinuate otherwise inadmissible evidence under the guise of cross-examination no longer have the right to elect whether or not to testify in their own behalf.[60]

This is because "the prosecutor can lay the predicate for admitting otherwise suppressible evidence with his own questioning."[61] More fundamentally, a decision like this "undercuts the constitutional canon that convictions cannot be procured by government lawbreaking."[62] The dissent noted the majority's reliance on a "completely freewheeling" balancing of police deterrence concerns against pursuit of truth concerns—an analysis common to all the decisions that undercut the exclusionary rule—"hardly conforms to the disciplined analytical method described as 'legal reasoning,' through which judges endeavor to formulate or derive principles of decision which can be applied consistently and predictably."[63] Finally, the dissent made it clear that it was disturbed by the majority's effort to "denigrate" *constitutional* protections in their quest to avoid application of the exclusionary rule.[64]

> Yet the efficacy of the Bill of Rights as a bulwark of our national liberty depends precisely upon public appreciation of the special character of constitutional prescriptions. The Court is charged with the responsibility to enforce constitutional guarantees; decisions such as today's patently disregard that obligation.[65]

Regardless, the Court invoked the impeachment exception again in *Michigan v. Harvey*,[66] where the Court allowed the government to impeach a defendant's trial testimony with a statement taken from him in apparent contravention of his Sixth Amendment rights.[67] In the earlier case of *Michigan v. Jackson*,[68] the Court stated police-initiated interrogation of counsel-represented defendants was an impermissible violation of the accused's right to counsel.[69]

However, in *Harvey* the Court took the position that where police circumvent an indicted defendant's determination to communicate with the police through counsel by initiating a private interview with him without counsel for the purpose of obtaining impeachment evidence, the fruits of their "end run" around counsel will be admissible to rebut the credibility of the defendant's trial testimony.[70]

Another significant restriction on the reach of the exclusionary rule is the standing doctrine. Since constitutional rights are personal rights[71] that may not be asserted vicariously by others,[72] a condition precedent to petitioning a court to suppress evidence is a demonstration on the part of a defendant that he is an "aggrieved" party.[73] If a defendant fails to show that his or her constitutional rights were implicated in the unconstitutional government activity, the defendant in question will have no basis to gain a suppression of the fruits of the illegal government action.[74]

During the Warren Era, the Court ruled that a person charged with a possessory offense had "automatic standing" regardless of where or from whom the contraband was seized.[75] A person "legitimately on premises" where evidence was seized unconstitutionally had standing to contest the search of the premises.[76] A person who had legal "custody" of an item could challenge the seizure of that item.[77] In the context of governmental electronic eavesdropping, the owner or tenant of the premises where illicit eavesdropping occurred had standing to challenge the eavesdropping that may have incriminated him even though he may not have been a party to the intercepted conversation and, as well, the parties to the conversation had the right to contest the surveillance in question.[78]

However, in 1978 the Burger Court issued the decision of *Rakas v. Illinois*,[79] where it reexamined the concept of standing and made it clear that it was prepared to find standing to advance a Fourth Amendment claim only where the defendant had a legitimate expectation of privacy in the area searched or items seized.[80] Furthermore, the Court held persons enjoy neither "vicarious" standing merely because the search infringed upon someone else's rights,[81] nor standing because they happened to be a "target" of the police search and seizure.[82]

Applying this privacy analysis in assessing whether a defendant was an aggrieved party in the case at hand, the *Rakas* Court determined that a mere passenger in an automobile belonging to another had no privacy interest in that automobile and, accordingly, no right to contest the unconstitutional search of that automobile.[83] The fact that the person was "legitimately" in the automobile was rejected as a basis for finding standing,[84] a basis that *was* accepted during the Warren Era.[85] Moreover, since the defendant had not asserted any legal interest in the items seized from the vehicle, he had no privacy interest that he could advance to contest the seizure of those items.[86]

Within a couple of years of *Rakas*, it became clear that the Court had considerably narrowed the concept of standing. In *United States v. Salvucci*,[87] the Court ruled that two defendants charged with criminal possession of certain matter had not demonstrated standing to object to the alleged illegal seizure of the matter from the home of one of the defendant's mother.[88] Here, the Court rejected the argument that the two defendants had "automatic" standing because they were charged with a possessory offense and, in the process, proclaimed the "automatic" standing rule had "outlived its usefulness."[89]

In *Rawlings v. Kentucky*,[90] they ruled a defendant had no standing to object to the search of a companion's purse that held his L.S.D.[91] Here, the accused was unable to demonstrate a legitimate expectation of privacy in his companion's purse.[92] Alternatively, the defendant was not entitled to challenge the search merely because he claimed ownership of the drugs in the purse because, the Court reasoned, "arcane" concepts of property law are not controlling in establishing a privacy interest in the item seized.[93] Thus, this case suggested that a defendant's claim of a possessory interest in the item seized would no more confer upon him standing than if, as in *Rakas*, he advanced no legal interest in the items seized by the police. Indeed, one might surmise from these cases that while standing might be established by an asserted interest in the *area* searched, it may be difficult or impossible to contest a search on an asserted interest in the *item* seized.

The same term the Court decided *Salvucci* and *Rawlings*, it also decided *United States v. Payner*,[94] which was even more intriguing. In *Payner*, the I.R.S. had launched an elaborate investigation of possible tax fraud of American citizens who had bank accounts in the Bahamas.[95] Eventually, suspicion focused on the Castle Bank in Nassau.[96] The I.R.S. used an informant, who cultivated a friendship with a Castle Bank executive in order to learn what he could about Castle Bank and its depositors.[97] Thereafter, the informant learned the Castle Bank executive was intending to spend several days in Miami and devised a scheme to gain access to bank records he knew the executive would be carrying.[98] Accordingly, the informant introduced the executive to a female informant.[99] When the executive and the female informant went out to dinner in Miami, the executive left his brief case behind in her apartment.[100] Thereafter, the original informant gained access to the female informant's apartment, removed the briefcase, delivered it to an I.R.S. agent who copied approximately 400 documents in the briefcase and, thereafter, returned the case to the apartment.[101] Within the briefcase were documents implicating the defendant.[102]

The federal district court determined that the government had deliberately violated the executive's privacy rights in order to obtain evidence against third parties, an effort that the district court characterized as a "knowing and purposeful *bad faith hostility* to any person's fundamental rights."[103] The district court concluded it was required to invoke due process and the inherent supervisory powers of the federal courts to exclude the documents implicating the defendant.[104]

However, the United States Supreme Court disagreed. Here, the Court held the defendant had no Fourth Amendment privacy interest in either the executive's briefcase or the bank's documents copied by the I.R.S. agent.[105] Furthermore, even if this government activity was "outrageous" in violation of due process, only the bank executive was an aggrieved party who had standing to complain.[106] Also, the Court rejected the district court's determination that it had the inherent supervisory power to suppress evidence seized unlawfully from a third party.[107] Finally, the Court returned to its now familiar cost-benefit analysis and, predictably, determined the cost of inadmissability outweighed the benefit of police deterrence.[108]

In a more recent case, *Minnesota v. Olson,*[109] the defendant was an overnight guest in an upstairs duplex where police conducted a warrantless arrest of him without exigent circumstances. [110] The Court held to "hold an overnight guest has a legitimate expectation of privacy in his host's home merely recognizes the everyday expectations we all share."[111] Whether *Olson* represents the Court's willingness to adopt a more moderate position on standing issues is by no means clear.

In any event, lower courts have followed the lead of the of the nation's highest court and have interpreted the standing doctrine very narrowly. For instance, in the automobile context, the lower appellate courts have found a defendant has no standing as a passenger in his mother's automobile[112] or where the defendant was a non-owner driver with the owner present.[113] In the residential setting, it has been held that an ordinary guest does not have standing to challenge the search of his host's dwelling,[114] and in a post-*Olson* decision, one court has ruled that even an "occasional" *overnight* has no privacy expectation in his host's residence sufficient to create standing to challenge an infringement upon his Fourth Amendment rights.[115]

The Burger and Rehnquist Courts have avoided the impact of the exclusionary rule in other ways. They ruled that where evidence was derived from an "independent source," it will be admissible, notwithstanding an earlier illegal search or seizure of the defendant.[116] The Courts also ruled that where the nexus between the initial illegal search and seizure and later discovered evidence arguably traceable to the initial search is weak, it will be admissible under the so-called "attenuation" doctrine.[117] While the "independent source" and "attenuation" doctrines enjoyed some support in Warren Court caselaw,[118] the Burger Court created a concept that provides if the evidence would have been eventually discovered by the police through legal means, it will be admitted by way of the so-called "inevitable discovery" concept.[119]

Another creation of the Burger Court was the so-called "good faith" exception to the exclusionary rule. It has been held that where a government agent seizes evidence pursuant to a warrant that is itself invalid[120] or seizes evidence with a facially valid warrant that was supported by an affidavit that failed to demonstrate probable cause,[121] and the officer executing the warrant harbors a "good faith" belief that his actions are legal, the evidence will be admissible. Where an officer is conducting a search under the authority of a statute later declared unconstitutional, the officer's good faith belief that his actions were legitimate will also save the evidence from suppression.[122] Again, the good-faith exception to the exclusionary rule had been utilized by the lower courts rather liberally. In one case, for example, the "good faith" concept saved the evidence from suppression where the police officer executed a warrant that was issued on the basis of an affidavit that the issuing judge had not even read.[123]

Finally, the United States Supreme Court under the tenure of Chief Justice Burger held that federal habeas corpus claims involving Fourth Amendment violations should not be relitigated in federal court where the state court system provided the state defendant a full and fair opportunity to litigate his claim.[124] The Court stated there was no advancement of a discernible benefit behind the exclusionary rule in reconsidering such claims in federal court.[125]

The myriad of exceptions and limitations placed on the exclusionary rule would seem to make little sense if the judiciary truly was bent on discouraging non-compliance with Fourth Amendment protections afforded the citizenry. Rather, it would appear that the courts could best accomplish that goal by not allowing for the likes of impeachment use of illegally seized evidence or by allowing the use of such evidence in grand jury inquiries. Similarly, it is rather odd that in the "good faith" decisions the Court concentrated only on the conduct of the police and casually ignored the inept performance of the respective judge's duties where, in one case, the judge issued a warrant on the basis of an affidavit not supported by probable cause[126] and where, in another case, the judge issued a facially invalid warrant.[127] However, by invoking the now familiar cost-benefit analysis theme, the United States Supreme Court allows for the admission of the constitutionally infirm evidence simply by stating that any potential police deterrence benefit is outweighed by the cost of losing otherwise reliable evidence of guilt.[128] In the end, the doctrinal limitations and exceptions have almost entirely swallowed the rule of exclusion. Thus, freedom from unconstitutional police action is sacrificed by a new balancing scheme that effectively posits that the costs of due process should not diminish the benefits of crime control.

It is noteworthy that most post-Mapp discussion of the appropriate reach of the exclusionary rule indicates the primary focus should be on the rule's deterrent effect on government misconduct.[129] The judicial integrity rationale is given only limited consideration.[130] Further, critics of the rule have complained that the application of the exclusionary rule has given rise to "tremendous costs on the judicial process."[131] These criticisms imply that if the exclusionary rule has no, or only a minimal, deterrent effect, it should be abolished.[132] Also, these objections suggest that, in any event, the exclusionary rule exacts too high a price from society, namely, "the release of countless guilty criminals."[133]

These criticisms require some scrutiny. In a study of the effects of the exclusionary rule in federal prosecutions conducted by the General Accounting Office,[134] it was discovered that in 2,804 cases under review, only 10.5 percent of all defendants filed a search and seizure motion to suppress,[135] in only 1.3 percent of these cases was evidence actually excluded,[136] and in only 0.4 percent of the cases were charges dropped because of suppression of the evidence.[137] Another study revealed that in California, only 2.4 percent of felony drug arrests were dropped by prosecutors because of illegal searches,[138] in only 0.6 percent of all homicide arrests were charges dropped for the same reason,[139] and only 1.0 percent to 2.0 percent of all rape, robbery, or assault arrests were not pursued because of the impact of the exclusionary rule.[140] A study in Illinois found that only 0.6 percent of all cases in a nine-county sample were lost because of the combined exclusions based on illegal searches, identifications, and confessions.[141] A study in Chicago reported that about 1.7 percent of all cases were lost because of the exclusionary rule, although most of these cases did not involve violent crime.[142] Meanwhile, regarding the deterrence issue, an empirical study of Chicago narcotics officers flatly stated in conclusion that "this study suggests the Supreme Court's skepticism concerning the deterrence rationale is unfounded."[143] These studies together seem to support the following conclusion: the exclusionary rule *does* act as a deterrent but *does not* exact a tremendous cost to society as is popularly perceived to be the case.

It is readily apparent to any student of criminal justice that the United States Supreme Court is not prepared to expand radically the reach of the exclusionary rule in order to deter official misconduct even further. On the other hand, the reported empirical studies may have taken the wind out of the sails of exclusionary rule critics who presume that the rule does not deter and that countless guilty defendants are being freed because of the rule's impact. Accordingly, abolitionist movements probably are unlikely to be successful in the foreseeable future.

What principle supports the existence of the current exclusionary rule, complete with all its exceptions and limitations? Clearly not deterrence, for, as stated earlier, if deterrence truly was the *paramount* concern, exceptions and limitations would not exist. Common sense alone supports the notion that the exclusionary rule would have its optimum deterrent effect if government officials realized that the fruits of their illegal evidence gathering would be useful in no judicial tribunal—not in preliminary examinations, trials for impeachment purpose, sentencing hearings, civil inquiries, and so forth. Similarly, if such barriers to application of the rule such as standing, good faith, and inevitable discovery were abolished, there would exist no incentive whatsoever to disregard this nation's charter. Thus, deterrence in reality is n*ot* the key justification for the exclusionary rule's existence.

It cannot be the "imperatives of judicial integrity" rationale that the Warren Court had in mind in *Mapp*. This becomes very evident in a review of exclusionary rule cases decided during the Burger and Rehnquist Court periods that (1) continually focus on the police deterrence rationale that is part and parcel of the cost-benefit analysis it utilizes to avoid application of the rule and (2) routinely ignore the judicial integrity argument found in *Mapp*. Furthermore, the Court's willingness to accept unconstitutionally seized evidence in our nation's *courts* in many more ways than was true in the past belies the notion that this Court is concerned about judicial integrity in the pure sense.

Rather, the Court's concern about its *own* image and the image of constitutional law *in the abstract* are the factors that most readily support the current doctrinal arrangement. If the Court abruptly walked away from the exclusionary rule, it would be seen as just another division of foot soldiers in a police state. If it became totally intolerant of police lawlessness, it would be accused of tolerance toward "common criminals," which would engender disrespect for the Court amongst the masses. Thus, the Court was determined to borrow the best from both worlds. On the one hand, they occasionally remind the citizenry as would Justice Brandeis, quoted at length in Mapp, that the government indeed is the "omnipresent teacher"[144] that must guide the populace by its example to a respect for law and, equally important, that a government beyond any check may one day drown in its own unconstitutional mire. Thus, the Justices keep the *general* rule intact to symbolize our societal disdain for the government as the lawbreaker and to placate our constant strive for freedom from government tyranny in a democratic society.[145] On the other hand, the Court allows the rule's exceptions and limitations to exist, as Justice Cardozo would have said, to ensure that merely because the constable blundered, the defendant should not necessarily be allowed to go free.[146] By avoiding application of the rule, the Court appears tough on crime. This arrangement, of course, cannot tolerate adherence to steadfast *principles* against government lawlessness.[147] Compromises, special exceptions and balancing tests are the order of the day. Judicial imagery replaces judicial integrity.

NOTES

1. 232 U.S. 383 (1914).
2. *Id.* at 393.
3. 367 U.S. 643 (1961).
4. *Id.* at 656 (quoting Elkins v. United States, 364 U.S. 206, 217 (1960)).
5. *Id.* at 659 (quoting Elkins v. United States, 364 U.S. 206, 222 (1960)).
6. *Id.* (quoting Olmstead v. United States, 277 U.S. 438, 485 (1928) (Brandeis, J., dissenting)).
7. Silverthorne Lumber Co., Inc. v. United States, 251 U.S. 385 (1920).
8. 414 U.S. 338 (1974).
9. *Id.* at 349–52 (incremental deterrent effect of extending exclusionary rule to grand jury uncertain). The Court attempted to distinguish *Silverthorne* by pointing out that Calandra had not been indicted. *Id.* at 352 n. 8.
10. *See, e.g.,* United States v. Graves, 785 F.2d 870 (10th Cir. 1986).
11. *See, e.g.,* United States v. Hill, 447 F.2d 817 (7th Cir. 1970).
12. *See, e.g.,* United States v. Fitzpatrick, 426 F.2d 1161 (2d Cir. 1970).
13. *See, e.g.,* People v. Grubb, 143 Ill.App.3d 822, 493 N.E.2d 699 (4th Dist. 1986).
14. *See* United States v. Calandra, 414 U.S. 338, 355–62 (Brennan, J., dissenting).
15. *See id.* at 365–67.
16. 380 U.S. 693 (1965).
17. *Id.* at 702.
18. *Id.* at 701–03.
19. *Id.* at 700. It should be noted that while the state could not retain the automobile because of the constitutional irregularity in the forfeiture proceeding, this decision does not mean a person can use the government's

unconstitutional seizure of contraband goods to gain return of contraband. *See* United States v. Jeffers, 342 U.S. 48 (1951) (narcotics); Trupiano v. United States, 334 U.S. 699 (1948) (illegal still and alcohol).

20. *See also* Boyd v. United States, 116 U.S. 616 (1986) (forfeiture proceeding wherein exclusionary rule applied).

21. 428 U.S. 433 (1976).

22. *Id.* at 459.

23. *Id.* at 434–36.

24. *Id.* at 437–38.

25. *Id.* at 436–37.

26. *Id.* at 438–39.

27. *See* notes 8–15 *supra* and accompanying text.

28. 428 U.S. at 453–54.

29. 428 U.S. at 463 (Stewart, J., dissenting).

30. 468 U.S. 1032 (1984).

31. *Id.* at 1050–51.

32. *Id.* at 1044.

33. *Id.* at 1048.

34. *Id.* at 1049.

35. *See, e.g., In re* Diane 110 A.2d 354, 494 N.Y.S.2d 881 (1985) (child protection inquiry); People v. Harfman, 638 P.2d 745 (Colo. 1981) (attorney disciplinary hearing).

36. *See* United States v. Havens, 446 U.S. 620 (1980); Harris v. New York, 401 U.S. 222 (1971).

37. *See* Walder v. United States, 347 U.S. 62 (1954); Agnello v. United States, 269 U.S. 20 (1925).

38. 269 U.S. 20 (1925).

39. *Id.* at 35.

40. 347 U.S. 62 (1954).

41. "It is one thing to say that the government cannot make an affirmative use of evidence unlawfully obtained. It is quite another to say that the defendant can turn the illegal method by which evidence in the government's possession was obtained to his own advantage, and provide himself with a shield against contradiction of his untruths." *Id.* at 65.

42. *Id.*

43. *Id.*

44. *Id.* at 66.

45. 401 U.S. 222 (1971).

46. 384 U.S. 436 (1966).

47. 401 U.S. at 225 (the "speculative possibility that impermissible police conduct will be encouraged thereby" is outweighed by the cost of exclusion).

48. Walder v. United States, 347 U.S. 62 (1954), was the only decision that had allowed the government to invoke the impeachment exception.

49. *See* 401 U.S. at 230, (Brennan, J., dissenting), quoting:

> The privilege against self-incrimination protects the individual from being compelled to incriminate himself in any manner . . . .[S]tatements merely intended to be exculpatory by the defendant are often *used to impeach his testimony at trial. . . . These*

> *statements are incriminating in any meaningful sense of the word and may not be used without the full warnings and effective waiver required for any other statement.* [Miranda v. Arizona,] 384 U.S. at 476–477 (emphasis added).

50. *See* 401 U.S. at 223.

51. 446 U.S. 620 (1980).

52. *Id*. at 622–23.

53. *Id*. at 623.

54. *Id*.

55. *Id*.

56. *Id*. at 625.

57. *Id*. at 627.

58. *Id*.

59. *Id*. at 630 (Brennan, J., dissenting), citing Walder v. United States, 347 U.S. 62, 66 (1954).

60. 446 U.S. at 629 (Brennan, J., dissenting).

61. *Id*. at 631.

62. *Id*. at 633.

63. *Id*. at 633–34.

64. *Id*. at 634.

65. *Id*.

66. 110 S. Ct. 1176 (1976).

67. *Id*. at 1180.

68. 475 U.S. 625 (1986).

69. *Id*. at 636.

70. *See* 110 S. Ct. at 1182–90 (Stevens, J., dissenting). It is noteworthy, however, that the Court in a recent 5–4 ruling determined that the impeachment exception to the exclusionary rule may not be used to impeach defense *witnesses* other than the defendant with unlawfully seized evidence. James v. Illinois, 110 S. Ct. 648 (1990).

71. *See* Rakas v. Illinois, 439 U.S. 128, 138 (1978) (Fourth Amendment rights are "personal" rights); Couch v. United States, 409 U.S. 322, 328 (1973) (Fifth Amendment privilege against self-discrimination is "personal" right).

72. Alderman v. United States, 394 U.S. 165, 174 (1969).

73. Jones v. United States, 362 U.S. 257, 265 (1960).

74. *See, e.g.,* Brown v. United States, 411 U.S. 223 (1973).

75. Jones v. United States, 362 U.S. 257, 263–65 (1960).

76. *Id*. at 267.

77. Mancusi v. Deforte, 392 U.S. 364, 369–70 (1968).

78. Alderman v. United States, 394 U.S. 165, 176 (1969).

79. 439 U.S. 128 (1978).

80. *Id*. at 148.

81. *Id*. at 133–38.

82. *Id*.

83. *Id*. at 148–49.

84. *Id*. at 140–48.

85. Jones v. United States, 362 U.S. 257 (1960).

86. 439 U.S. at 148.

87. 448 U.S. 83 (1980).
88. *Id.* at 95.
89. *Id.*
90. 448 U.S. 98 (1980).
91. *Id.* at 106.
92. *Id.* at 104–06.
93. *Id.* at 105.
94. 447 U.S. 727 (1980).
95. *Id.* at 729.
96. *Id.*
97. *Id.* at 729–30.
98. *Id.* at 730.
99. *Id.*
100. *Id.*
101. *Id.*
102. *Id.*
103. *Id.* at 730–31.
104. *Id.* at 731.
105. *Id.* at 731–32.
106. *Id.* at 737, n. 9.
107. *Id.* at 733–37.
108. *Id.*
109. 110 S. Ct. 1684 (1990).
110. *Id.* at 1686–87.
111. *Id.* at 1689.
112. People v. Coleman, 146 Ill.App.3d 806, 489 N.E.2d 455 (2d Dist. 1986).
113. United States v. Lochan, 674 F.2d 960 (1st Cir. 1982); People v. Flowers, 111 Ill.App.3d 348, 444 N.E.2d 242 (2d Dist. 1982).
114. People v. Cohen, 146 Ill.App.3d 618, 494 N.E.2d 1231 (2d Dist. 1986).
115. People v. Cortis, 237 Neb. 97, 465 N.W.2d 132 (1991).
116. Murray v. United States, 108 S. Ct. 2529 (1988); United States v. Crews, 445 U.S. 463 (1980).
117. *See* New York v. Harris, 110 S. Ct 1640 (1990); United States v. Ceccolini, 435 U.S. 268 (1978); People v. Gabbard, 78 Ill. 2d 88, 398 N.E.2d 574 (1979).
118. *See* Wong Sun v. United States, 371 U.S. 471 (1963).
119. Nix v. Williams, 467 U.S. 431 (1984).
120. Massachusetts v. Sheppard, 468 U.S. 981 (1984).
121. United States v. Leon, 468 U.S. 897 (1984).
122. Illinois v. Krull, 480 U.S. 340 (1987).
123. United States v. Breckenridge, 782 F.2d 1317 (5th Cir. 1986).
124. Stone v. Powell, 428 U.S. 465, 481–82, 494 (1976).
125. *Id.* at 493–94.
126. United States v. Leon, 468 U.S. 879, 916–917 (1984) (suppressing evidence obtained pursuant to subsequently invalidated warrant penalizes officer for magistrate's error and will not deter Fourth Amendment violations by police).

127. Massachusetts v. Sheppard, 468 U.S. 981, 990 (1984) (suppressing evidence because magistrate erred ill-serves deterrent function).

128. *See, e.g.*, United States v. Ceccolini, 435 U.S. 268, 273, 276–77 (1978) (application of exclusionary rule to live witness testimony erroneous since deterrent effect is speculative); United States v. Janis, 428 U.S. 433, 453–54 (1976) (illegally seized evidence admissible in federal civil proceedings since societal costs of exclusion outweigh deterrent effect).

129. *See, e.g.*, Illinois v. Krull, 480 U.S. 340, 347 (1987) ("prime purpose" of exclusionary rule is to deter "future unlawful police conduct").

130. *See, e.g.*, Stone v. Powell, 428 U.S. 465, 485–86 (1976) (dictum) (judicial integrity rationale has only limited force as justification for exclusion of highly probative evidence).

In United States v. Leon, 468 U.S. 897 (1984), the Court suggested that the judicial integrity rationale was subsumed in the deterrence rationale: "whether the use of illegally obtained evidence in judicial proceedings represents judicial participation in a Fourth Amendment violation and offends the integrity of the courts 'is essentially the same as the inquiry into whether exclusion would serve a deterrent purpose.'" *Id.* at 921 n. 22 (quoting United States v. Janis, 428 U.S. 433, 459 n. 35 (1976)).

131. California v. Minjares, 443 U.S. 916, 919 (Rehnquist, J., with Burger, C.J., dissenting from denial of stay), *cert. denied*, 444 U.S. 887 (1979). *See also* Stone v. Powell, 428 U.S. 465, 496–502 (1976) (Burger, C.J., concurring) (exclusionary rule imposes tremendous costs on society and neither protects judicial integrity nor deters official misconduct).

132. Bivens v. Six Unknown Named Agents, 403 U.S. 388, 416 (1971) (Burger, C. J., dissenting) ("[t]here is no empirical evidence to support the claim that the rule actually deters illegal conduct of law enforcement officials") (citing Dallin Oaks, *Studying the Exclusionary Rule in Search and Seizure*, 37 U. CHI. L. REV. 665, 667 (1970)); Coolidge v. New Hampshire, 403 U.S. 443, 491 (1971) (Harlan, J., dissenting) ("[T]he assumed 'deterrent value' of the exclusionary rule has never been adequately demonstrated . . .").

133. Bivens v. Six Unknown Named Agents, 403 U.S. 388, 416 (1971) (Burger, C.J., dissenting).

134. Report of the Comptroller General of the United States, Impact of the Exclusionary Rule on Federal Criminal Prosecutions Rep. No. CDG-79–45 (April 19, 1979).

135. *Id.* at 8.

136. *Id.* at 11.

137. *Id.* at 14.

138. Thomas Davies, *A Hard Look at What We Know (and Still Need to Learn) About the "Costs" of the Exclusionary Rule: The NIJ Study and Other Studies of "Lost Arrests,"* 1983 AM. B. FOUND. 611, 618 (1983).

139. *Id.* at 645.

140. *Id.*

141. Peter Nardulli, *The Societal Cost of the Exclusionary Rule: An Empirical Assessment*, 1983 AM. B. FOUND. 585, 606 (1983).

142. Peter Nardulli, *The Societal Cost of the Exclusionary Rule Revisited*, 1987 U. ILL. L. REV. 223, 234–36 (1987). *See also* Joseph Tybor & Mark

Eissman, *Illegal Evidence Throws Out Few Cases*, CHI TRIBUNE, Jan. 5, 1986, at sec. 1, p. 1.

143. Comment, *The Exclusionary Rule and Deterrence: An Empirical Study of Chicago Narcotics Officers*, 54 U. CHI. L. REV. 1016, 1054 (1987).

144. Mapp v. Ohio, 367 U.S. 643, 659 (1961) (quoting Olmstead v. United States, 277 U.S. 438, 485 (1928) (Brandeis, J., dissenting)).

145. *Id.*

146. People v. Defore, 242 N.Y. 13, 21, 150 N.E. 585, 587 (Cardozo, J.), *cert. denied*, 270 U.S. 657 (1926).

147. *See generally* Yale Kamisar, *Does (Did)(Should) the Exclusionary Rule Rest on A "Principled Basis" Rather Than an Empirical Proposition?"* 16 CREIGHTON L. REV. 565 (1983).

Chapter 3

Fourth Amendment Protections: "Public Exposure" Reasoning and "Reasonableness" Exposed

THE FOURTH AMENDMENT was designed to protect people, their houses, and personal effects from unreasonable searches and seizures, and, on its face, it states seizures of persons or their property require the issuance of a judicial warrant based on probable cause.[1] In interpreting this amendment, the Warren Court not only reaffirmed the Court's long-standing strong preference for searches made pursuant to a warrant,[2] but it also indicated warrantless searches and seizures are "per se unreasonable," subject to carefully drawn exceptions.[3] The Court stated "police must, whenever practicable, obtain advance judicial approval of searches and seizures. . . ."[4] Furthermore, in *Katz v. United States*,[5] discussed in Chapter 1,[6] the Court abandoned the narrow "trespass" on "property" analysis that had previously governed the question as to whether a government "search" had occurred and therein defined a search as an infringement of a citizen's subjective expectation of privacy that society is prepared to consider reasonable.[7]

Katz seemed to be a clear effort on the part of the Warren Court to broaden Fourth Amendment protections stating it was designed to protect "people" and their reasonable expectations of privacy rather than mere "places."[8] In *Katz*, the Court determined the defendant had a reasonable expectation of privacy even in his conversations inside a public telephone booth.[9] In that case, the Court held the government's warrantless electronic surveillance of the telephone booth was invasive of the defendant's "privacy," even if not his "property."[10] However, the *Katz* opinion added: "What a person *knowingly exposes to the public* even in his own home or office, is not a subject of Fourth Amendment protection."[11] Here the Court was stating the obvious: if a person openly exposes his activities in a fashion that he knows will be within public view, he should not be able to complain that his privacy was invaded if it turned out a police officer was nestled amongst the public, who were able to see or hear the defendant's open activities. In other words, the Court was suggesting that if Katz had been screaming at the top of his voice in an open telephone booth in a crowded area, with the result that someone nearby overheard Katz's incriminating statements, he would not be able to assert that his listener had invaded his privacy. Similarly, the Court was implying that if Katz had openly displayed what was clearly contraband from within his glass telephone booth to passersby outside, he could not object to the passersby's failure promptly to close their eyes and look the other way. In the case at hand, in contrast, the defendant had, in the opinion of the Court, sought to exclude the "uninvited ear" of all as he spoke in normal voice within the confines of the phone booth unaware of a hidden listening device intercepting his conversation.[12]

Thus, what might be described as the "public exposure" doctrine[13] was developed. However, in the discussion that follows, it will be demonstrated how the "public exposure" concept has been stretched beyond all logic and reason by the Burger and Rehnquist Courts. In a variety of settings, those Courts have relied on the public exposure doctrine to justify the conclusion that there was *no* "search" for Fourth Amendment purposes, even though the government action in the case at hand clearly amounted to a deliberate effort to gain evidence of criminality from an unsuspecting citizen. Specifically, the Court does this via a three-step process. First, the Court manages to find some type of "exposure" of the incriminating matter to someone—and n*ot* necessarily the *public* at large. The exposure is often minuscule in nature and r*arely* can be classified as *knowingly* on the part of the subject under scrutiny. Second, the Court determines where there is "exposure," there can be *no* legitimate privacy interest. And, finally, the Court concludes where no privacy interest exists, there was no "search."

A second significant aspect of contemporary Fourth Amendment jurisprudence is the United States Supreme Court's utilization of a "reasonableness" analysis.[14] Here, the Court emphasizes that the Constitution prohibits not all warrantless searches, but only "unreasonable searches."[15] In this connection, the Court invokes a balancing test that weighs the defendant's privacy interest against the state's interest in effective law enforcement.[16] For example, where the government interest in detecting crime is great and the privacy interest is relatively minimal, the reasonableness test may allow for warrantless searches[17] and seizures[18] on a "reasonable suspicion"[19] rather than on "probable cause," which is the only test for evaluating the legitimacy of a search or seizure specifically mentioned in the Constitution. An excellent illustration of the reasonableness approach is *Terry v. Ohio.*[20] In that case, the Warren Court ruled that a suspect, whom the police had no probable cause to arrest, could be subjected to a stop and frisk for weapons on the basis of a reasonable suspicion to believe he was armed and dangerous.[21] Here, the Court ruled that concerns over the officer's safety outweighed the suspect's right to be entirely free of a search and seizure.[22]

But again, as with the "public exposure" concept, the Burger and Rehnquist Courts have used the "reasonableness" standard in a fashion that hardly could have been imagined by the members of the Warren Court majority.[23] Most significantly, the reasonableness standard has been used in post-Warren Court opinions to uphold warrantless searches[24] and seizures[25] even where the government agent had no individualized suspicion whatsoever.[26] Thus, in *New York v. Class*,[27] the United States Supreme Court upheld a police officer's action of reaching into an automobile, involved in mere traffic violations, in order to move papers which obstructed the officer's view of the vehicle identification number situated on the vehicle's dashboard.[28] Although it was "undisputed that the police officer had no reason to suspect that the respondent's car was stolen, that it contained contraband, or that the respondent had committed an offense other than the traffic violation,"[29] the Court upheld the officer's "search."[30] The Court reasoned that the intrusion was minor and clearly was outweighed by the police officer's interest in highway safety and the officer's personal security.[31]

Both the "public exposure" doctrine and the "reasonableness" analysis may have some place in Fourth Amendment inquiries. However, both concepts have been very broadly interpreted by the Supreme Court in the past twenty years with the concomitant result that certain commentators have felt forced to observe that the nation is facing an incredibly shrinking Fourth Amendment protection.[32] Numerous critics have observed, in one or more connections, that many of the Supreme Court's decisions regarding the Fourth Amendment are seriously flawed.[33] There exists strong support for such conclusions.

1. *The "Public Exposure" Concept*

The Court's contemporary use of the "public exposure" concept is relatively simple. As alluded to above, where the Court finds some type of exposure of the incriminating matter to someone, their finding completely defeats a person's privacy expectation, which, in turn, leads the Court to conclude there was no government search. Some critics indicate that the Court appears to be rather confused about semantics;[34] others cynically view these decisions as a deliberate step in an

Orwellian direction.[35] A cursory review of recent cases illustrates the Court's constant temptation to utilize that doctrine in order to conclude that there "was no 'search' within the meaning of the Fourth Amendment."[36] For example, in *Oliver v. United States*,[37] in one broad sweep the Court ruled landowners *never* have an expectation of privacy in so-called "open fields."[38] Here, the Court upheld police passage through "no trespassing" signs and entry into fenced parcels of land while bent on finding marijuana.[39] The Court could not surmise how a person could *ever* have an expectation of privacy on his lands[40] beyond the curtilage, which is the protected area immediately surrounding his residence,[41] even though the dissent reminded the majority that

> Privately owned woods and fields that are not exposed to public view regularly are employed in a variety of ways that society acknowledges deserve privacy. Many landowners like to take solitary walks on their property, confident that they will not be confronted in their rambles by strangers or policemen. Others conduct agricultural businesses on their property. Some landowners use their secluded spaces to meet lovers, others to gather together with fellow worshippers, still others to engage in sustained creative endeavor. Private land is sometimes used as a refuge for wildlife, where flora and fauna are protected from human intervention of any kind.[42]

Remarkably, the Court in *Oliver* stated that Fourth Amendment protection has nothing to do with civil trespass concerns.[43] But more remarkable was the Court's proposition that merely because enclosed lands *might be observable* from the exterior, that gave the police carte blanche authority to *gain entry*.

In *United States v. Dunn*,[44] the Court outlined what constituted a curtilage[45] and, predictably, viewed it as having not been invaded where federal agents entered a defendant's ranch, which was completely encircled by a perimeter fence, crossed interior fences, shined lights inside a barn situated approximately fifty yards from the residence of the ranch, and observed a drug manufacturing operation within.[46] Here, neither the area beyond the series of fences nor the barn itself were viewed as within the ranch's curtilage.[47] This case suggests a property owner might only be able to argue convincingly the existence of a curtilage protected from government entry if the area in question is within very close proximity to his residence and the area, including the residence, is surrounded by a high wall, sufficiently solid to exclude observations from the outside, that is liberally covered with "Private Property—Keep Out" signs.[48]

Following *Oliver*, the Court invoked the open fields doctrine to uphold various types of aerial surveillance. In *California v. Ciraolo*,[49] the Court held the Fourth Amendment was not violated when government agents flew over the defendant's enclosed backyard at an altitude of 1,000 feet.[50] Ciraolo had erected two fences around his backyard, a six-foot outer fence and a ten-foot inner fence, to protect his backyard from observation on the ground.[51] While the Court conceded that the backyard, which contained marijuana plants, fell within the defendant's curtilage, the officer had a right to make *observations* from outside assuming he was in an area where he had a right to be.[52] Here, the Court held that the officer had a right to be in the open airspace above the defendant's curtilage.[53]

In a companion case to *Ciraolo*, the Court ruled in *Dow Chemical v. United States*,[54] that Environmental Protection Agency aerial photography of a chemical plant to gain evidence of the emission of pollutants was constitutional even though the plant was protected by elaborate ground security that barred public view of the plant.[55] In addition, in *Florida v. Riley*,[56] the Court ruled police observation of marijuana within a partially covered greenhouse situated on a residential curtilage through the use of a helicopter circling at an altitude of 400 feet was permissible since the helicopter was within navigable airspace over the property.[57] Thus, it appears our hypothetical landowner will only be guaranteed complete privacy from government scrutiny of his curtilage if he builds a solid dome over the area in question. In any event, a review of the "open fields" case law, which includes the aerial surveillance decisions, demonstrates how the Court effectively uses the public exposure concept to defeat privacy claims.

The Court's creative use of the public exposure theory does not end with the open fields cases. For example, in *United States v. Place*,[58] the Court ruled that the use of police dogs that undertake a "canine sniff" of luggage in an airport does not constitute a "search" within the contemplation of the Fourth Amendment.[59] Since the owner of the luggage exposed the luggage (and the odors emanating therefrom) to public scrutiny, his privacy claim was rejected.[60]

In *Texas v. Brown*,[61] the Court ruled that a police officer's use of a flashlight to light the interior of an automobile's glove compartment, in circumstances where the car had been stopped at a driver's license checkpoint, did "not constitute a search."[62] Here, the illuminated area was observable from outside the automobile "by either inquisitive passersby or diligent police officers."[63]

In *California Banker's Association v. Schultz*[64] and *United States v. Miller*,[65] the Court held that a person's banking records do not enjoy privacy. In *Miller* the Court stated:

All documents obtained, including financial statements and deposit slips, contain only information voluntarily conveyed to the banks and *exposed* to their employees in the ordinary course of business. * * * The depositor takes the risk, in *revealing* his affairs to another, that the information will be conveyed by that person to the government.[66]

In *New York v. New York Telephone Company*[67] and *Smith v. Maryland*,[68] the Court ruled the government's use of pen registers, which are mechanical devices that record all numbers dialed on a telephone by monitoring the electrical impulses of the dialing mechanism, was not invasive of privacy. In *Smith*, the Court stated: "When he used his phone, [Smith] *voluntarily conveyed* numerical information to the telephone company and '*exposed*' that information to its equipment in the ordinary course of business. In so doing, [Smith] assumed the risk that the company would reveal to police the numbers he dialed."[69]

Another sophisticated electronic sense enhancing device sanctioned by the United States Supreme Court in certain circumstances is the electronic beeper tracking device.[70] A "beeper" is a radio transmitter, usually battery operated, that silently emits periodic signals that can be picked up by a radio receiver.[71] In *United States v. Knotts*,[72] government authorities suspected certain defendants were purchasing chloroform to be used in the manufacture of illicit drugs.[73] Without court approval but with the consent of a chemical company from which one of the defendants was purchasing chloroform, the government agents hid a beeper in a five-gallon container of chloroform that eventually was picked up by one of the defendants.[74] Through the use of this device, the government was able to monitor the movement of the container to outside a secluded cabin not previously known to the authorities.[75] Based on this information, plus three days of visual surveillance of the cabin, the authorities procured a search warrant and discovered a drug manufacturing operation within.[76]

Eventually, the Supreme Court upheld the government use of the beeper device against the defendants' claim of privacy.[77] The Court reasoned that a person traveling on a public thoroughfare has no expectation of privacy in his movement from one place to another since "he voluntarily conveyed to anyone who wanted to look" his direction, stops, and ultimate destination.[78] Regarding the use of the beeper that went beyond the capabilities of any visual surveillance, "[n]othing in the Fourth Amendment prohibited the police from augmenting the sensory faculties bestowed upon them at birth with such enhancement as science and technology afforded them in this case."[79]

In a later case, the Supreme Court held that beeper monitoring in a residence was invasive of privacy since activities behind closed doors are not exposed to the public.[80] In any event, *Knotts* presents an excellent example of the public exposure concept at work.

Returning to more conventional government inquiries, the Court has ruled an employee may not necessarily have a reasonable expectation of privacy in his workplace environment where the area in question is open to others,[81] that a homeowner never has a reasonable expectation of privacy in the trash containers he places at the curbside outside his residence,[82] and that a shopkeeper has no reasonable expectation of privacy as to the wares he displays on the shelf of an adult bookstore.[83] Nor, as *United States v. Dunn* made clear, does one have a reasonable expectation of privacy from police observations of activities within a building partially open to outside observation, assuming the officer is stationed in an area where he has a right to be.[84]

Following the lead of the United States Supreme Court, many lower appellate courts have liberally construed the "public exposure" concept. For example, it has been held that a defendant relinquished objective privacy expectations from police surveillance when he left his window drapes partially open and had his window covered only by sheer curtains;[85] when he left his window open;[86] when he left a hole in contact paper covering his window that was sufficiently large to allow observations from a public passageway;[87] when he opened the door to his house;[88] when he opened his garage door;[89] when he sat in a windowed motor vehicle with contraband on his lap;[90] when he traversed through an apartment building's common hallway behind a locked outer door;[91] when he spoke loud enough in a hotel room to be heard by a government agent in an adjoining room who was listening through a hole in the wall;[92] when his conversations were overheard by agents in an adjoining hotel room who pressed their ears against a common door;[93] when his telephone message clearly was audible, through speakers on a telephone answering machine, to agents lawfully on the premises;[94] when his telephone conversations were monitored by an agent's listening in on a "party line";[95] when his ham radio conversations were intercepted;[96] when his telephone conversation on a cordless telephone was monitored on an ordinary AM radio receiver;[97] when his activities in his home were observable by an agent standing on a stepladder using binoculars;[98] when contraband on a plane parked on a runway at a public airport was visible to an agent standing on a stepladder looking into the plane;[99] when his contraband was visible through a louvered opening in a greenhouse through the use of binoculars, night vision lenses, and telephoto lenses;[100] when his person was visible outside a building through the use of a nightscope;[101] when his plane's movement was monitored by a beeper tracking device, which movement otherwise could have been detectable by visual and radar tracking;[102] when his activities in his residence were capable of being photographed through the use of a telephoto lens;[103] when a person was subjected to a canine sniff;[104] when a shopper's body was screened by a sensormatic device that would reveal whether she was stealing merchandise from the store;[105] when a defendant's apartment, which contained a large quantity of stolen watches containing luminous, radium-treated dials, was monitored by a scintillator, which measures radiation, that was situated outside the apartment in a public hallway;[106] when a defendant left a packet of cocaine under a doormat in front of his apartment;[107] when his fourth-class mail parcels, which could be opened by postal authorities to determine if size, weight, and content conformed with postal regulations, was opened by postal authorities at the behest of the police;[108] and when his activities and movements were subjected to constant police surveillance.[109]

It is difficult to surmise that the average lay person appreciates the extent to which they may lose their constitutional protection against government scrutiny by failing to isolate themselves and their activities completely from public view. The Court's reasoning in this connection seems more akin to protecting those who might chose to maintain a hermitage existence in a cave than the rest of us who prefer the political, social, and economic intercourse of modern society.

2. The "Reasonableness" Standard

The reasonableness standard of the Fourth Amendment generally has been interpreted as requiring a warrant based on probable cause before a search or seizure is permitted.[110] The reasonableness test requires balancing of law enforcement interests against citizen privacy interests in each case.[111]

In some cases, the reasonableness test may be violated even where the authorities have a warrant based on probable cause.[112] On the other hand, the reasonableness test may require only a warrant based on a watered-down version of probable cause;[113] only probable cause and not a warrant;[114] neither a warrant nor probable cause, and only a "reasonable" suspicion;[115] or nothing in the way of an individualized suspicion.[116]

One might not quibble with the exceptions to the warrant requirement, for often it is not practical to procure a warrant.[117] In that connection, the Court has approved a number of exceptions to the warrant clause, namely, exigent circumstances,[118] hot pursuit,[119] searches incident to an arrest,[120] seizures of items in plain view,[121] searches of vehicles,[122] inventory searches,[123] consent searches,[124] border searches,[125] searches on the high seas,[126] and searches of heavily regulated businesses to assure compliance with government regulations that are designed to protect the public's health and safety.[127]

More troublesome, however, is the erosion of the probable cause standard as it gradually is being replaced by a reasonable suspicion test in many settings.[128] For instance, an investigatory stop of an automobile on a public thoroughfare[129] or of a pedestrian in a public place[130] is permissible on a reasonable suspicion. More importantly, the United States Supreme Court has indicated it is permissible on a reasonable suspicion to *search* a suspect for weapons,[131] a high school student's purse for contraband,[132] a probationer's home for contraband,[133] and an employee's workplace.[134] In each instance, the Court tilted the scales of the balancing test in favor of the government.[135]

And most disconcerting is the Court's willingness to tolerate searches or seizures without any individualized suspicion.[136] For example, the Court has upheld the search of a car for its vehicle identification number[137] and the removal of a person from his automobile[138] without any suspicion whatsoever.

The best example of how the reasonableness test can justify an essentially standardless governmental inquiry arose in two 1989 United States Supreme Court opinions dealing with drug testing. In *National Treasury Employees v. Von Raab*[139] and *Skinner v. Railway Labor Executives Association*,[140] the Court approved of drug testing of certain railway employees and certain federal customs agents, respectively, without any individualized suspicions that the persons being tested were actually under the influence of intoxicants. In *Skinner*, federal law mandated the blood and urine tests of railway employees, such as the operators of locomotives, following a train accident.[141] After reviewing the significant number of train accidents, fatalities, injuries, and dollars lost as a consequence of railway employee on-the-job intoxication,[142] the Court employed the reasonableness test,[143] weighed the government interests against the employees' privacy interests,[144] and determined that the warrant requirement, probable cause test, and the reasonable suspicion standard would impede the governments interest in railway safety.[145] The Court concluded the toxicological testing did not constitute an undue infringement on the privacy of the covered employees even though they be carried out where there was no suspicion the respective employees were actually intoxicated.[146]

Similarly, in *Von Raab* the Court upheld a suspicionless drug testing program instituted by the U.S. Customs service that was directed at customs employees involved either in the interdiction of drugs being smuggled into the country or in the handling of firearms.[147] Interestingly, Justice Scalia wrote a scathing dissent in *Von Raab*.[148] He pointed out that unlike the railway industry, where a history of train accidents traceable to on-the-job intoxication had been demonstrated by the government, the Customs Service appeared to be largely drug free.[149] He noted the decision to impose drug testing was essentially based on the Custom Service's interest in setting an "example" in the war against drugs.[150] He then responded to this supposed justification:

> What better way to show that the Government is serious about its "war on drugs" than to subject its employees on the front line of the war to this invasion of their privacy and affront to their dignity? To be sure, there is only a slight chance that it will prevent some serious public harm resulting from Service employee drug use, but it will show to the world that the Service is "clean," and—most important of all—will demonstrate the determination of the Government to eliminate this scourge of our society! I think it obvious that this justification is unacceptable; that the impairment of individual liberties cannot be the means of making a point; that symbolism, even symbolism for so worthy a cause as the abolition of unlawful drugs, cannot validate an otherwise unreasonable search.

> *   *   *

> Those who lose because of the lack of understanding that begot the present exercise in symbolism are not just the Customs Service employees, whose dignity is thus offended, but all of us—who suffer a coarsening of our national manners that ultimately give the Fourth Amendment its content, and who become subject to the administration of federal officials whose respect for our privacy can hardly be greater than the small respect they have been taught to have for their own.[151]

Yet, the majority ruled. Justice Scalia's position did not prevail. The "war on drugs" approved in *Von Raab* may have been little more than a symbolic exercise, but the majority apparently concluded this symbolism to be a worthy exercise. Again, the clang of the symbols coming from those in the crime control establishment was louder than that emanating from the corner of those who cry out for due process. The Court thought it better to place limits on rights *against* searches than on the power to search. The Court believed it is better for us to be drug free than to be free.

3. *Automobile Stops and Searches: An Illustration*

Beyond the Burger and Rehnquist Courts' freewheeling use of the public exposure doctrine and reasonableness test, the demise of Fourth Amendment protection becomes quite apparent by reviewing one particular context where searches and seizures are quite common: the automobile situation. A police stop ordinarily necessitates only a reasonable suspicion.[152] Moreover, in a roadblock setting no individualized suspicion is required.[153] In any event, probable cause is not required to justify the stop.

Assuming the automobile is properly stopped and a custodial arrest for a traffic infraction occurs, the arrestee can be searched for contraband even though the search in question could not have yielded a weapon or evidence supportive of the arrest.[154] Moreover, the search incident to the arrest may extend *beyond* those areas that are actually within the arrestee's reach.[155] The search incident to the arrest doctrine originally was designed to allow police only to search an arrestee for weapons or other destructible evidence within his reach.[156] The Burger Court later ruled this doctrine could be used to search the entire passenger compartment of the automobile and all enclosed areas or containers within the automobile, such as the glove compartment or luggage, even though the arrestee was outside of his car and not within actual reach of the area in question.[157] Some lower courts have interpreted this case law as authority for invoking the search incident to the arrest concept to justify the search of the interior of an automobile, even where the defendant is situated in a police car in handcuffs.[158] These holdings simply cannot be squared with the rationale behind the search incident to the arrest doctrine. Where the weaponry or other evidence clearly is outside the defendant's reach and the police, who generally are armed themselves, obviously have total dominion and control over the defendant and his automobile, the search incident to the arrest concept is being stretched beyond all logic and reason. Expediency in law enforcement wins out at all cost.

Long ago the Court recognized that where the police have seized an automobile on a public thoroughfare, in circumstances where they have probable cause to believe it contains contraband or other evidence of a crime, they can conduct a warrantless search immediately because the automobile's inherent mobility on the public thoroughfare makes it impracticable to secure a warrant.[159] More significantly, however, a group of Burger Court opinions hold that where the police do not immediately conduct a curbside search of the vehicle that they have grounds to search but instead take exclusive custody of the vehicle and remove it to the police station, their search at the latter location without a warrant is permissible.[160] In one case, for example, the Court sustained a warrantless search of an automobile that had been impounded eight hours earlier and was presently located in a secure area.[161] These latter decisions seem ludicrous since they are at odds with the principle that it was "not practicable to secure a warrant because the vehicle can be quickly moved out of the locality or jurisdiction in which the warrant is sought."[162] If the authorities clearly had time to get a warrant to search the impounded vehicle, their failure should not be excused.[163]

Further, where the police are faced with a hybrid situation, such as a camper or motor-home that might be likened to a residence, the automobile exception to the warrant clause wins out.[164] Thus, where the police had probable cause to search a "mini" motor home situated in a parking lot, their warrantless search was upheld by the Court despite the absence of any specific exigent circumstances.[165]

The tendency on the part of the United States Supreme Court to avoid the warrant clause in the automobile context is perhaps best illustrated by *United States v. Ross*[166] and *California v. Acevedo*.[167] In two earlier cases,[168] the Court held where the police had probable cause to believe contraband was situated in luggage about to be placed in an automobile[169] or that already had been placed in an automobile,[170] the police needed a warrant to open the luggage that they had seized and that was now in their "exclusive control."[171] The Court reasoned that each of the luggage containers was a "repository of personal effects" deserving of privacy in a manner not enjoyed by an automobile.[172] In a later case, the Court stated two packages wrapped in green opaque plastic were to be afforded the protection of the "container" cases while rejecting the government's argument that some containers might not be worthy of protection.[173]

In *Ross*, police learned from an informant that the defendant was selling narcotics kept in the trunk of his car that was parked at a specific location.[174] The police immediately drove to the location, found the car, arrested and handcuffed the defendant, and searched the trunk.[175] In the trunk, the police found a closed paper bag that contained heroin and a zippered leather pouch that contained a large amount of cash.[176] Later, the defendant apparently contended that even if the police could conduct a warrantless search of the trunk, they could not open the containers without a warrant.[177] In response, the *Ross* Court stated that where the focus of the probable cause determination was a *container* coincidentally situated in an automobile, then this "repository of personal effects" could only be opened with a warrant, assuming it is in the officers' exclusive control.[178] However, if the police focus was on the *entire vehicle* or, in other words, they had probable cause to believe the contraband was *somewhere* within the auto, then they could conduct a warrantless search of the entire vehicle and all containers within the vehicle under the automobile exception to the warrant requirement.[179] This distinction developed in *Ross* gave rise, therefore, to the incredible proposition that the less the police knew about specific whereabouts of contraband situated in an automobile, the greater their authority to search any containers in it. Moreover, since the police in *Ross* had been advised that the defendant was selling narcotics out of his trunk and, accordingly, the focus of the police search was on the trunk itself, then why was the trunk not treated as a repository of personal effects? Obviously, notwithstanding contrary pronouncements from the Court,[180] after *Ross* some containers were more unworthy of the warrant clause protection than others.

Nine years after *Ross*, the Court attempted to undo the confused state of the law regarding searches of a container located in an automobile where the police believe the container holds contraband. In *California v. Acevedo*,[181] police observed defendant leaving an apartment, known to contain marijuana, carrying a paper bag that they had reason to believe contained marijuana.[182] After the defendant placed the bag in the trunk of his automobile and began to drive off, the police stopped defendant's auto, opened the trunk and the bag, and found marijuana.[183] Because the police focus regarding the marijuana was on the paper bag specifically rather than the entire automobile, the California Court of Appeals ruled the warrantless search of the bag was unconstitutional and the marijuana should have been supressed.[184] The United States Supreme Court reversed, observing:

> Until today, this Court has drawn a curious line between the search of an automobile that coincidentally turns up a container and the search of a container that coincidentally turns up in an automobile. The protections of the Fourth Amendment should not turn on such coincidences.[185]

The *Acevedo* Court held searches of automobile should be governed by "one rule."[186] The police would now be permitted to conduct a warrantless search of an automobile and any container within it so long as they have probable cause to believe the contraband or evidence is contained in the auto or container.[187]

While *Acevedo* might be praised for its elimination of the "curious" distinction raised in *Ross*, or condemned because it allows warrantless searches of "repositories of personal effects" where it may be practical to get a warrant, the decision presents another anomaly. Since *Acevedo* does away with the protection of a warrant previously afforded a container in the automobile context but let stand the protection of a warrant afforded a container outside the automobile setting, Fourth Amendment jurisprudence now prohibits "a search of a briefcase while the owner is carrying it exposed on a public street" but permits a warrantless search "once the owner has placed the briefcase in the locked trunk of his car."[188]

Beyond the search incident to the arrest doctrine and probable cause plus automobile exception approaches, the authorities have other bases for searching an automobile. Where the police have a reasonable suspicion that an occupant of a car may have weaponry in an automobile, they can invoke the stop and frisk doctrine to search the suspect,[189] the entire passenger compartment, and all containers therein.[190] Again, the area searched, as with the search incident to an arrest, does not actually have to be within the physical reach of the suspect.[191]

Finally, the police have the right to "inventory" a lawfully impounded automobile.[192] Obviously, the police might impound an automobile in a variety of settings: after a roadside arrest and detention of the automobile's occupants; following an accident; where a motorist with automobile mechanical problems temporarily abandons his vehicle on the roadside where it poses a possible hazard; where a motorist temporarily abandons his automobile in inclement weather; where a motorist parks his car in a towaway zone; or where the police order a car to be towed to a car pound because of previous unpaid tickets for parking violations. In any event, an inventory of a vehicle in police custody has been upheld because of three distinct justifications: (1) protection of the owner's property, (2) protection of the police from civil claims of lost or stolen property, and (3) protection of the police and public from potentially dangerous articles located in the car.[193]

An inventory can extend to the trunk and other containers in the vehicle.[194] Further, the police need not allow the owner or driver to make other arrangements for safekeeping his property because the Court has ruled that the police are not required to employ the "least intrusive" means of protecting the property.[195] Finally, inventories are not dependent on probable cause or a warrant since the police motivation is not discovery of contraband or evidence of a crime.[196]

A review of the Fourth Amendment protection, or lack thereof, that surrounds a motor vehicle illustrates how a curious, inventive police officer has a variety of concepts he can rely on to justify his scrutiny of the contents of an automobile. The old adage, "if there is a will, there is a way" may not be terribly far from reality in this setting. The same might be said in other settings beyond automobiles. While the case law regarding other settings could be explored, it is not the point of this exercise to review the failing of all the Fourth Amendment decisions decided by the Supreme Court of the United States. Rather, it is to demonstrate how Fourth Amendment protection have been narrowed to such an extent that in many situations they become almost meaningless.

4. A Final Comment

One problem with current Fourth Amendment jurisprudence is the entire inconsistency of the public exposure doctrine and the reasonableness model. Reasonableness analysis weighs the privacy interests of the citizen and balances law enforcement interest against the citizen's claim of privacy. The greater the privacy interest, the less likely the law enforcement actions will be tolerated unless stringent standards be satisfied that justify the invasion of the citizen's zone of privacy. Where the privacy interest is minimal, then the hurdles the government must overcome to accomplish their objectives are significantly lowered. Thus, a sort of sliding scale governs the reasonableness analysis. In sharp contrast, the "public exposure" concept relies on an opposite approach.

> To label any police activity a "search" or "seizure" within the ambit of the amendment is to impose . . . restrictions upon it. On the other hand, if it is not labeled a "search" or "seizure" [because of public exposure considerations], it is subject to no restrictions of any kind. It is only "searches" or "seizures" that the fourth amendment requires to be reasonable: police activities of any other sort may be as unreasonable as the police please to make them.[197]

What is left is a "kind of all-or-nothing" approach.[198] Why is the "public exposure" test not subject to a sliding scale?[199] One could utilize, as one commentator has suggested, such an analysis by considering (1) the risk of public exposure, (2) the extent of the public exposure, and (3) to whom the citizen has exposed his activities or items.[200] As to the first point, should the citizen who stands in his secluded residence before an open window at 3:00 in the morning face the same risk of public exposure as the person who is situated behind a window in his street-level business on a heavily traveled street at 3:00 in the afternoon? As to the second point, has the homeowner who is standing behind a window with curtains drawn except for a two-inch gap between the curtains exposed his actions to the public to the same degree as the homeowner who has not drawn his curtains at all? And, regarding the third point, where a homeowner chooses not to draw his curtains to exclude his next-door neighbor's view of the interior of his residence, should this mean that he has no right to object to police telescope surveillance of his residence interior that is conducted from a substantial distance away?

Here, it would seem logical to rule on a case-by-case basis that where the risk of and degree of exposure to many is great, the police power to look should be subject to minimal standards. Where the exposure is very limited in terms of risk, extent and persons, then the government's actions would require satisfaction of a much higher standard. Other considerations might be relevant in such an analysis as well. For example, where a police officer uses a sophisticated mechanical viewing device to *deliberately* subject a homeowner's activities to his scrutiny, should he not be subject to a different standard than the officer on street patrol who *inadvertently* sees homeowner mischief with his naked eye from a sidewalk outside the residence? The failure of the Court to consider such factors in its "privacy" inquiry is difficult, if not impossible, to defend.

Another criticism can be directed at the public exposure test appears if one considers the origin of the test, namely, *Katz* itself. The Warren Court stated what one "knowingly" exposes to the public is not within a zone of privacy.[201] One might ask if an agent is peering through a resident's partially shaded window in the night time with a nightscope or flashlight in hand, how can it be said that the resident "knowingly" exposed his affairs to another, particularly where he believed he had accomplished his goal of excluding the uninvited eye by turning out the interior lights in his dwelling place?

Of course, once a "search" or "seizure" does come into play, the courts do weigh a number of variables in assessing whether the warrant requirement, probable cause standard, the reasonable suspicion test or the no individualized suspicion approach applies. Here, a balancing of interests approach *is* utilized in assessing the reasonableness of the government's actions. But, again, criticisms can be directed at the current *application* of the "reasonableness" standard to various situations. Returning to the automobile stop, search and seizure caselaw, the difficulties can be readily observed. Where the police stop an automobile because of their belief that the automobile driver is subject to an outstanding arrest warrant for murder, should they be allowed to conduct their stop consistent with the same standard they are allowed to use to stop a person for a burned-out tail light? Perhaps the stop of the murder suspect involves a greater law enforcement interest than the stop of the driver with the malfunctioning tail light and, accordingly, ought to be subject to a lesser standard. Or perhaps, since the level of intrusiveness following the stop of the murder suspect will likely be far greater than their stop of the driver who ordinarily will be only "ticketed" for a motor vehicle violation and, accordingly, the former situation should require a higher standard than the latter. However, no principled difference between these two situations is attempted or discussed in the caselaw.

In the automobile context where the police have probable cause to believe contraband is present, no distinction is made between the situation where an automobile is on an open highway where it may be truly impractical to procure a warrant and the impounded automobile situation where it is clearly possible to get a warrant. In the search-incident-to-the arrest caselaw, no distinction is made between the custodial arrest for a motor vehicle violation and the custodial arrest of a criminal. Here, the Court affords the police the same power to search the custodial arrestee after the traffic infraction that they extend to the police to search an arrested murderer. In addition, the Court deliberately eviscerated the distinction between the police necessity to search a passenger compartment incident to an arrest whether or not the arrestee is *in fact* within reach of a weapon or destructible evidence. Similarly, the power to "frisk" the automobile passenger compartment for weapons exists regardless of whether the area in question is *in reality* within reach of a suspect. And the *necessity* for an inventory is ignored in those situations where the police have no legitimate reason to continue to hold an automobile and the automobile owner is prepared to take alternative measures for safekeeping of his automobile. In all of these situations, it is difficult to identify the law enforcement interest that *necessitates* the dismissal of the privacy interest *except police expediency* which, of course, the courts will not articulate as a justification. In other words, if it is not necessary to stop a car in certain circumstances on less than probable cause, then how can the stop be considered reasonable? If it is not necessary to search a car without a warrant, then how can the warrantless search be reasonable? If it is not possible for a custodial arrestee situated outside a car to destroy evidence in the car, how can the search be squared with the reasonableness standard? If the suspect standing away from his stopped automobile has no opportunity to grab a weapon, how can the "frisk" of the car interior be justified? And if it is not necessary to "inventory" an automobile for the owner's safekeeping, why is the government action reasonable?

By adopting a simplistic approach as to what constitutes "public exposure," the Court has abandoned the purpose of this concept. By giving into government claims of law enforcement necessity in circumstances where there actually existed no compelling necessity for the police intrusion, the "reasonableness" standard becomes meaningless. What, then, does the future hold?

Fourth Amendment protection never will become entirely extinct because of the constitutional amendment process or judicial interpretation. They will remain, to some extent, to symbolize our freedom from police excesses and undue government scrutiny of citizen affairs. The Court will continue to entertain and review claims of Fourth Amendment violations to assure the citizenry that it is taking seriously its role as guardian of the Constitution.[202]

And to the extent affected individuals complain about government overreaching into their private affairs, the Court will attempt to soothe the rest of us into complacency by reminding us that both it and the police were doing only that which was required to protect us from drug peddlers, murderers, and other misfits. In each and every case, it will quote all or, at least a portion, of the Fourth Amendment to remind us of our security from government snooping. In virtually every case, it will state that the warrant requirement and probable cause test is the standard that normally is to be employed in assessing the propriety of a police search and seizure and, thereafter, as it suits the Court's convenience, invoke this or that exception or the doctrine in order to conclude all was fair and reasonable. The private citizen's conviction is affirmed. The lip service given to the Fourth Amendment provides the masses security from the government. The affirmance offers society security from the convicted criminal. A happy compromise has been reached. Everyone is pleased . . . until it is the window of their life that the police are looking through. At that juncture, the citizen will ask, like the law student who is first exposed to a Fourth Amendment hypothetical in criminal procedure or constitutional law, "They can't do that, can they?"

NOTES

1. U.S. CONST. Amend. IV.
2. *See, e.g.*, United States v. Ventresca, 380 U.S. 102, 105–07 (1965).
3.

> [I]t is a cardinal principle that "searches conducted outside the judicial process, without prior judicial approval by judge or magistrate, are *per se* unreasonable under the Fourth Amendment— subject only to a few specifically established and well delineated exceptions."

Katz v. United States, 389 U.S. 347, 357 (1967).
4. Terry v. Ohio, 392 U.S. 1, 20 (1968).
5. 389 U.S. 347 (1967).
6. *See* Ch. 1, notes 12–26 and accompanying text.
7. 389 U.S. at 361 (Harlan, J., concurring).

8. *Id.* at 351.

9. *Id.* at 352 (defendant had a reasonable expectation of privacy from the government's "uninvited ear").

10. *Id.* at 352–53.

11. *Id.* at 351 (emphasis added).

12. *Id.* at 352. The Warren Court had indicated it was prepared to use an "exposure" analysis where the suspect *did realize* that his incriminating statements were being heard by his listener. For instance, in Lopez v. United States, 373 U.S. 427 (1963), a defendant had attempted to bribe an Internal Revenue Service agent in order to conceal his tax liability. *Id.* at 429–30. In a subsequent conversation with the agent, the defendant's incriminating statements were recorded by a tape recorder concealed on the agent's person. *Id.* at 430–32. The Court held the warrantless use of the device did not infringe on Fourth Amendment protections since "the risk that petitioner took in offering a bribe . . . fairly included the risk that the offer would be accurately reproduced in court, whether by faultless memory or mechanical recording." *Id.* at 439. Similarly, in United States v. White, 401 U.S. 745 (1971), a government informer carrying a radio transmitter engaged the defendant in a conversation which was overheard by government agents using a radio receiver. *Id.* at 746–47. The informer was not produced at trial, but the testimony of the "eavesdropping" agent was admitted at trial. *Id.* at 747. The Court held that the government activity, for constitutional purposes, was no different than in *Lopez*, even if the agent not actually present during the conversation instead had recorded the transmitted statements. *Id.* at 751.

13. Charles Whitebread & Christopher Slobogin, CRIMINAL PROCEDURE, sec. 4.02(b) (2d ed. 1986).

14. *See, e.g.*, New York v. Class, 475 U.S. 106 (1986) (officer's reaching into car involved in traffic violation in order to move papers obstructing view of vehicle identification number not unreasonable considering minor intrusion and lesser expectation of privacy in automobile).

15. *See, e.g.*, Terry v. Ohio, 392 U.S. 1, 16–31 (1968) (stop and frisk of suspect for weaponry on less than probable cause was reasonable).

16. *See id.* at 22–27 (suspect's privacy interests outweighed by officer's safety). *Compare* United States v. Place, 462 U.S. 696, 703 (1983) (seizure of defendant's luggage for ninety minutes outweighs law enforcement concerns).

17. *See, e.g.*, T.L.O. v. New Jersey, 469 U.S. 325 (1985) (search of high school student's purse justified on reasonable suspicion given problem of criminality in schools).

18. *See, e.g.*, Delaware v. Prouse, 440 U.S. 648 (1979) (stop of automobile on reasonable suspicion justified given diminished expectation of privacy in automobile context).

19. *See supra* notes 15–18.

20. 392 U.S. 1 (1968).

21. *Id.* at 30–31.

22. *Id.* at 22–27.

23. For example, Justice Marshall conceded in Adams v. Williams, 407 U.S. 143, 161–62 (1972) (Marshall, J., dissenting), that experience with the stop and frisk concept had proven to him he was mistaken when he had voted

with the majority in Terry v. Ohio, 392 U.S. 1 (1968), wherein the Court had used the reasonableness analysis to uphold the stop and frisk concept.

24. *See, e.g.*, New York v. Class, 475 U.S. 106 (1986).

25. *See, e.g.*, Michigan Department of State Police v. Sitz, 110 S.Ct. 2481 (1990) (stop of automobile and brief examination of drivers to determine if intoxicated at roadblock sobriety checkpoints requires no individualized suspicion); Pennsylvania v. Mimms, 434 U.S. 106 (1977) (ordering driver stopped for traffic violation out of car amounts to seizure but requires no individualized suspicion); United States v. Martinez-Fiord, 428 U.S. 543 (1976) (stop of automobile and questioning of occupants at permanent checkpoints requires no individualized suspicion).

26. *See supra* notes 24–25.

27. 475 U.S. 106 (1986).

28. *Id.* at 107.

29. *Id.* at 108.

30. *Id.* at 115.

31. *Id.* at 117–19.

32. Silas J. Wasserstrom, *The Incredible Shrinking Fourth Amendment*, 21 AM. CRIM. L. REV. 257 (1984).

33. John M.A. DiPippa, *Is the Fourth Amendment Obsolete?—Restating the Fourth Amendment in Functional Terms*, 22 GONZAGA L. REV. 483 (1987/ 88); Charles Whitebread & John Heilman, *The Counter-revolution Enters a New Era: Criminal Procedure During the Final Term of the Burger Court*, 10 U. PUGET SOUND 571 (1987); Wayne LaFave, *The Forgotten Motto of Obsta Principiis in Fourth Amendment Jurisprudence*, 28 ARIZ L. REV. 291 (1986); Yale Kamisar, *"Comparative Reprehensibility" and the Fourth Amendment Exclusionary Rule*, 86 MICH. L. REV. 1 (1987); Stephen A. Saltzburg, *Another Victim of Illegal Narcotics: The Fourth Amendment (as illustrated by the open fields doctrine)*, 48 U. PITT. L. REV. 1 (1986); Harry M. Caldwell, *Seizures of the Fourth Kind: Changing the Rules*, 33 CLEV. ST. L. REV. 323 (1984–85); J. Michael Hunter & Paul R. Joseph, Illinois v. Gates: *A Further Weakening of Fourth Amendment Protection*, 6 U. BRIDGEPORT L. REV. 19 (1985).

34. Clark D. Cunningham, *A Linguistic Analysis of the Meanings of "Search" in the Fourth Amendment: A Search for Common Sense*, 73 IOWA L. REV. 541 (1988).

35. John M. Burkoff, *When is a Search Not A "Search?" Fourth Amendment Doublethink*, 15 U. TOLEDO L. REV. 515 (1984).

36. *See, e.g.*, United States v. Place, 462 U.S. 696, 707 (1983) (canine sniff of luggage in airport not a "search").

37. 466 U.S. 170 (1984).

38.

> [O]pen fields do not provide the setting for those intimate activities that the Amendment is intended to shelter from government interference or surveillance. There is no society interest in protecting

> the privacy of those activities, such as the cultivation of crops, that occur in open fields. Moreover, as a practical matter these lands usually are accessible to the public and police in ways that a home, an office or commercial structure would not be. It is not generally true that fences or "No Trespassing" signs effectively bar the public from viewing open fields in rural areas.

Id. at 179.

39. *Id.* at 182–84.
40.

> Nor would a case-by case approach provide a workable accommodation between the needs of law enforcement and the interests protected by the Fourth Amendment. Under this approach, police officers would have to guess before every search whether landowners had erected fences sufficiently high, posted a sufficient number of warning signs, or located contraband in an area sufficiently secluded to establish a right to privacy.

Id. at 181.

41. *Id.* at 180.
42. *Id.* at 192 (Marshall, J., dissenting).
43. [T]he common law of trespass furthers a range of interests that have nothing to do with privacy. . . . [T]he law of trespass confers protection from intrusion by others far broader than those required by Fourth Amendment interests.
Id. at 183–84 n. 15.
44. 480 U.S. 294 (1987).
45. The Court identified four factors that would be used in identifying the existence of a curtilage: (1) proximity of the area to a residence; (2) whether the area was included within an enclosure surrounding the residence; (3) the nature of the uses to which the area is put; and (4) the steps taken by the resident to protect the area from observation from outside. *Id.* at 301.
46. *Id.* at 301–03.
47. *Id.*
48. It is highly doubtful the average American would have the resources or proclivity to isolate oneself in this manner.
49. 476 U.S. 207 (1986).
50. *Id.* at 215.
51. *Id.* at 209.
52. *Id.* at 212–14. This right to observe does not necessarily mean there automatically exists a right to enter, for, unlike "open fields" that the officer has a right to enter, the backyard being within the curtilage was within a constitutionally protected area.
53. *Id.* at 213.
54. 476 U.S. 227 (1986).
55. *Id.* at 236–39.
56. 109 S. Ct. 693 (1989).
57. *Id.* at 696–97.
58. 462 U.S. 696 (1983).
59. *Id.* at 707.

60. *Id.* The Court eventually ruled, however, the government's retention of the defendant's luggage for ninety minutes while awaiting the canine sniff was an excessive time in the absence of probable cause. *Id.* at 709–10.

61. 460 U.S. 730 (1983) (plurality).

62. *Id.* at 740.

63. *Id.*

64. 416 U.S. 21 (1974).

65. 425 U.S. 435 (1976).

66. *Id.* at 442–43 (emphasis added).

67. 434 U.S. 159 (1977).

68. 442 U.S. 735 (1979).

69. *Id.* at 744 (emphasis added).

70. United States v. Karo, 468 U.S. 705 (1984); United States v. Knotts, 460 U.S. 276 (1983).

71. United States v. Knotts, 460 U.S. 276, 277 (1983).

72. 460 U.S. 276 (1983).

73. *Id.* at 278.

74. *Id.*

75. *Id.* at 277–79.

76. *Id.* at 279.

77. *Id.* at 285.

78. *Id.* at 281–82.

79. *Id.* at 282.

80. In United States v. Karo, 468 U.S. 705 (1984), government agents suspected various defendants were intending to use ether in their processing of cocaine. *Id.* at 708. With the consent of an informer who was supplying defendants with the ether, a beeper was placed in a fifty-gallon drum of the substance. The informer delivered the container to Caraway, and through the use of the beeper, the government was able to establish that it was in Caraway's residence. Later, through the use of the beeper, it was determined that the container was moved to Horton's residence. Two days later, it was discovered that the ether was moved again and, using the device, agents established it was in Horton's father's house. In the ensuing day, the ether was moved to a storage facility, a second storage facility, a residence belonging to Rhodes, and finally, to a residence in Taos, New Mexico, where evidence of drug processing was discovered through the use of a search warrant. *Id.* at 708–10.

    The Court ruled that the monitoring of the beeper inside a residence, a location not open to visual surveillance, is violative of privacy for the "beeper tells the agent that a particular article is actually located at a particular time in the private residence and is in the possession of the person or persons whose residence is being watched." *Id.* at 715. This situation was different from that in *Knotts* since in that case the beeper that found its way to out*side* the secluded cabin "told the authorities nothing about the interior" whereas here "the monitoring indicated that the beeper was inside the house, a fact that could not have been visually verified." *Id.* Thus, where the beeper verified the presence of the ether in the Taos house that ultimately was searched, that evidence would be inadmissible, but only as to "those with privacy interests in the house." *Id.* at 719. Even those who had a privacy interest in the Taos house would not necessarily have standing to object to the movement of the ether to and through other person's homes or storage facilities. *Id.* at 719–20. Also, since the truck that brought the ether to the Taos house had traversed upon a public thoroughfare, *Knotts* would allow that information to be used in support of the warrant that authorized the search of the house. *Id.* at 721. And, since there was sufficient information in the affidavit for issuance of the search warrant, after striking the information gained from the monitoring that continued *after* the ether was removed from the truck into the house, that pointed to the presence of contraband in the Taos house, the search of the house was proper. *Id.* at 724.

81. *See* O'Conner v. Ortego, 480 U.S. 709 (1987) (plurality opinion):

> [S]ome government offices may be so open to fellow employees or the public that no expectation of privacy is reasonable. * * * Given the great variety of work environments in the public sector, the question of whether an employee has a reasonable expectation of privacy must be addressed on a case-by-case basis.

Id. at 718.

82. California v. Greenwood, 108 S. Ct. 1625 (1988):

> It is common knowledge that plastic bags left on or at the side of a public street are readily accessible to animals, children, scavengers, snoops and other members of the public.

Id. at 1628–29.

83. Maryland v. Macon, 472 U.S. 463, 469 (1985).

84. United States v. Dunn, 480 U.S. 294, 304 (1987) (quoting California v. Ciracolo, 476 U.S. 207, 213 (1986)):

> [T]he Fourth Amendment "has never been extended to require law enforcement officers to shield their eyes when passing by a home on public thoroughfares."

85. State v. Thompson, 196 Neb. 55, 241 N.W.2d 511 (1976) (observation permissible).

86. People v. Wright, 41 Ill. 2d 170, 242 N.E.2d 180, *cert. denied*, 395 U.S. 933 (1969) (observation permissible).

87. United States v. Acevedo, 627 F.2d 68, 69 n. 1 (7th Cir.), *cert. denied*, 449 U.S. 1021 (1980) (observation permissible).

88. State v. Rodriguez, 653 S.W.2d 305 (Tex. Crim. App. 1983) (observation and entry permissible).

89. People v. Hobson, 169 Ill. App. 3d 485, 525 N.E.2d 895 (1st Dist. 1988) (observation and entry permissible).

90. People v. Rhoades, 74 Ill. App. 3d 247, 392 N.E.2d 923 (4th Dist. 1979) (observation permissible). *See also* United States v. Head, 783 F.2d 1422 (9th Cir. 1986) (agent's peering through van's darkened windows, while cupping his hands around his eyes to exclude the glare from exterior lights, was not invasive of privacy).

91. United States v. Holland, 755 F.2d 253 (2d Cir. 1985) (tenant's arrest without warrant permissible since no reasonable expectation existed that officer not be in hallway).

92. United States v. Mankini, 738 F.2d 538 (2d Cir. 1985) (agent's pressing of ear to pre-existing hole in common wall to overhear conversations in adjoining room permissible).

93. United States v. Agapito, 620 F.2d 324 (2d Cir. 1980) (aural surveillance permissible).

94. United States v. Whitten, 706 F.2d 1000 (9th Cir. 1983), *cert. denied,* 465 U.S. 1100 (1984) (aural surveillance).

95. Lee v. State, 191 So. 2d 84 (Fla. App., 4th Dist. 1966) (aural surveillance permissible).

96. United States v. Rose, 669 F.2d 23 (1st Cir.), *cert. denied,* 459 U.S. 828 (1982) (aural surveillance permissible).

97. State v. Howard, 235 Kan. 236, 679 P.2d 197 (1984) (aural surveillance permissible).

98. Commonwealth v. Hernley, 216 Pa. Super. 177, 263 A.2d 904 (1970), *cert. denied,* 401 U.S. 914 (1971) (observation permissible).

99. United States v. Bellina, 665 F.2d 1335 (4th Cir. 1981) (observation permissible).

100. Wheeler v. State, 659 S.W. 381 (Tex. Crim. App. 1982) (observation permissible).

101. United States v. Ward, 703 F.2d 1058 (8th Cir. 1983) (observation permissible).

102. United States v. Parks, 684 F.2d 1078 (5th Cir. 1982) (monitoring of plane's movement permissible).

103. State v. Louis, 296 Or. 57, 672 P. 2d 708 (1983) (photo observation permissible).

104. Doe v. Renfrow, 475 F. Supp. 1012 (N.D. Ind. 1979), *aff'd in part and rev'd in part,* 631 F.2d 91 (7th Cir. 1980) (per curiam) (body search reasonable but nude body search unreasonable).

105. Lucas v. United States, 411 A.2d 360 (D.C. App. 1980) (monitoring permissible).

106. Corngold v. United States, 367 F.2d 1 (9th Cir. 1966) (scintillator monitoring permissible).

107. People v. Shorty, 731 P.2d 679 (Colo. 1987) (search and seizure permissible; not within "curtilage").

108. Commonwealth v. Dembo, 451 Pa. 1, 301 A.2d 689 (1973) (search and seizure reasonable).

109. Weber v. City of Cedarburg, 129 Wis. 2d 57, 384 N.W.2d 333 (1986) (surveillance permissible).

110. *See, e.g.,* Payton v. New York, 445 U.S. 573 (1980) (entry of arrestee's home for purpose of effectuating an arrest required an arrest warrant based on probable cause); Johnson v. United States, 330 U.S. 10 (1948) (entry of hotel room to seize opium required search warrant based on probable cause).

111. Camara v. Municipal Court, 387 U.S. 523, 536–37 (1967).

112. Winston v. Lee, 470 U.S. 753, 759 (1985) (court-ordered surgery to remove bullet from defendant unreasonable since no compelling evidentiary need for bullet existed).

113. *See, e.g.,* Camara v. Municipal Court, 387 U.S. 523 (1967) (administrative search of residence requires probable cause although probable cause can be

demonstrated without showing specific reason to believe code violation exists within residence).

114. *See, e.g.*, California v. Carney, 471 U.S. 386 (1987) (search of motor home does not require a warrant because of inherent mobility of vehicle and diminished expectation of privacy associated with motor vehicles).

115. *See, e.g.*, Griffin v. Wisconsin, 483 U.S. 868 (1987) (warrantless search of home of probationer permissible since probable cause and warrant requirement "impractical" in state's probation system).

116. *See, e.g.*, New York v. Class, 475 U.S. 106 (1986) (entry of motor vehicle to move papers covering vehicle identification number requires no individualized suspicion).

117. *See, e.g.*, Schmerber v. California, 384 U.S. 757 (1966) (not practical to procure warrant to remove blood from drunk driver given inevitable dissipation of driver's blood alcohol level).

118. *See, e.g., id.*

119. *See, e.g.*, United States v. Santana, 427 U.S. 38 (1976); Warden v. Hayden, 387 U.S. 294 (1967).

120. *See, e.g.*, New York v. Belton, 453 U.S. 454 (1981); United States v. Robinson, 414 U.S. 218 (1973).

121. *See, e.g.*, Horton v. California, 110 S. Ct. 2301 (1990).

122. *See, e.g.*, California v. Carney, 471 U.S. 386 (1987).

123. *See, e.g.*, Colorado v. Bertine, 479 U.S. 367 (1987); South Dakota v. Opperman, 428 U.S. 364 (1976).

124. *See, e.g.*, Illinois v. Rodriguez, 110 S. Ct. 2793 (1990); Schneckloth v. Bustamonte, 412 U.S. 218 (1973).

125. United States v. Montoya de Hernandez, 473 U.S. 531 (1985); United States v. Ramsey, 431 U.S. 606 (1977).

126. United States v. Villamonte-Marquez, 462 U.S. 579 (1983).

127. New York v. Burger, 482 U.S. 691 (1987).

128. *See infra* notes 129–35 and accompanying text.

129. United States v. Sharpe, 470 U.S. 675 (1985); Delaware v. Prouse, 440 U.S. 648 (1979).

130. United States v. Sokolow, 109 S. Ct. 1581 (1989).

131. Adams v. Williams, 407 U.S. 143 (1972).

132. New Jersey v. T.L.O., 469 U.S. 325 (1985).

133. Griffin v. Wisconsin, 483 U.S. 868 (1987).

134. O'Connor v. Ortega, 480 U.S. 709 (1987) (plurality opinion).

135. *See* New Jersey v. T.L.O., 469 U.S. 325, 352 (1985) (Blackmun, J., concurring) (concerned that balancing test has become the rule rather than the exception).

136. *See, e.g.*, Michigan Department of State Police v. Sitz, 110 S. Ct. 2481 (1990) (temporary stop of automobile at sobriety checkpoint).

137. New York v. Class, 475 U.S. 106 (1986).

138. Pennsylvania v. Mimms, 434 U.S. 106 (1977).

139. 109 S. Ct. 1384 (1989).

140. 109 S. Ct. 1402 (1989).

141. 109 S. Ct. at 1407, referring to the Federal Railroad Safety Act of 1970, 45 U.S.C. sec. 431(a).

142. 109 S. Ct. at 1407–08.
143. *Id.* at 1413–14.
144. *Id.* at 1414–21.
145. *Id.*
146. *Id.* at 1421–22.
147. *Id.* at 1397. However, the Court refused to decide whether a third class of employees—those handling "classified" information—could be similarly tested since the lower court record was inadequate. *Id.* at 1398.
148. *Id.* at 1398–1402 (Scalia, J., dissenting).
149. *Id.* at 1400.
150. *Id.*
151. *Id.* at 1401–02.
152. Delaware v. Prouse, 440 U.S. 648, 663 (1979).
153. Micigan Department of State Police v. Sitz, 110. S. Ct. 2481 (1990).
154. United States v. Robinson, 414 U.S. 218 (1973) (search of cigarette packet of person arrested for driving without a valid driver's license upheld).
155. New York v. Belton, 453 U.S. 454 (1981).
156. *See* Chimel v. California, 395 U.S. 752 (1969).
157. 453 U.S. at 460–61.
158. People v. Loftus, 111 Ill. App. 3d 978, 444 N.E.2d 834 (4th Dist. 1983).
159. Carroll v. United States, 267 U.S. 132, 153 (1925).
160. Texas v. Brown, 423 U.S. 67 (1975) (at-the-station search of vehicle after occupants arrested and taken into custody upheld); Chambers v. Maroney, 399 U.S. 42 (1970) (warrantless search of automobile after occupants had been arrested and taken into custody and where automobile had been removed from curbside to police station permissible).
161. Florida v. Meyers, 466 U.S. 380 (1984) (per curiam).
162. This principle, referred to as the "*Carroll* doctrine," is derived from Carroll v. United States, 267 U.S. 132, 153 (1925).
163. *See* Vivian D. Wilson, *The Warrantless Automobile Exception: Exception Without Justification,* 32 HAST. L. J. 127 (1980).
164. California v. Carney, 471 U.S. 386 (1987).
165. *Id.* at 394.
166. 456 U.S. 798 (1982).
167. 111 S. Ct. 1982 (1991).
168. Arkansas v. Sanders, 442 U.S. 753 (1979); United States v. Chadwick, 433 U.S. 1 (1977).
169. United States v. Chadwick, 433 U.S. 1 (1977).
170. Arkansas v. Sanders, 442 U.S. 753 (1979).
171. 433 U.S. at 15. *See also* 442 U.S. at 763–64.
172. 433 U.S. at 13. *See also* 442 U.S. at 764–65.
173. Robbins v. California, 453 U.S. 420, 426–27 (1981) (plurality opinion).
174. 456 U.S. at 800.
175. *Id.* at 801.
176. *Id.*
177. *See id.* at 801–03 (discussion of "container" decisions).
178. *Id.* at 809–17.
179. *Id.* at 817–25.

180. Robbins v. California, 453 U.S. 420, 426–27 (1981) (plurality opinion).
181. 111 S. Ct. 1982 (1981).
182. *Id.* at 1984.
183. *Id.* at 1984–85.
184. *Id.* at 1985.
185. *Id.* at 1991.
186. *Id.*
187. *Id.*
188. *Id.* at 2001 (Stevens, J., dissenting).
189. Adams v. Williams, 407 U.S. 143 (1972).
190. Michigan v. Long, 463 U.S. 1032 (1982).
191. *Id.* at 1048–52.
192. South Dakota v. Opperman, 428 U.S. 364 (1976). However, the inventory practices of a police department must be consistent with standardized procedures. Florida v. Wells, 110 S. Ct. 1632 (1990).
193. *Id.* at 369.
194. Colorado v. Bertine, 479 U.S. 367 (1987).
195. *Id.* at 373–74.
196. *Id.* at 371–73.
197. Anthony G. Amsterdam, *Perspectives on the Fourth Amendment*, 58 MINN. L. REV. 349, 388 (1974).
198. *Id.*
199. *Id.* at 390.
200. Brian J. Serr, *Great Expectations of Privacy: A New Model of Fourth Amendment Protection*, 73 MINN. L. REV. 583, 633–39 (1989).
201. Katz v. United States, 398 U.S. 347, 351 (1967).
202. Even this proposition may be somewhat suspect. In *Michigan v. Long*, 463 U.S. 1032 (1983), Justice Stevens castigated the Burger Court majority on this point:

> I believe that in reviewing the decisions of state Courts, the primary role of this Court is to make sure that persons who seek to *vindicate* federal rights have been fairly heard. * * *
>
> Until recently we had virtually no interest in cases [where the state was asking for a reversal of state Court finding favorable to a state petitioner which finding may have been based on an independent state ground]. Thirty years ago, this Court reviewed only one. * * * Fifteen years ago, we did not review any such cases, although the total number of requests had mounted to three. Some time during the past decade . . . our priorities shifted. The result is a docket swollen with requests by states to reverse judgments that their courts have rendered in favor of their citizens. [Citation to thirteen cases which the Court agreed to hear during the 1982–83 term] I am confident that a future Court will recognize the error of this allocation of resources.
>
> When that day comes, I think it likely that the Court will also reconsider the propriety of today's expansion of our jurisdiction.

Id. at 1068–70 (Stevens, J., dissenting).

In 1991, Justice Stevens made a comparable attack on the Rehnquist Court majority. In *California v. Acevedo*, 111 S. Ct. 1982 (1991), he discussed the Court positions in narcotics cases over a nine-year period:

In the [past nine] years . . . , the Court has heards arguments in 30 Fourth Amendment cases involving narcotics. In all but one, the government was the petitioner. All save two involved a search or seizure without a warrant or with a defective warrant.

And, in all except three, the Court upheld the constitutionality of the search or seizure. * * * [D]ecisions like the one the Court makes today will support the conclusion that this Court has become a loyal foot soldier in the executive's fight against crime.

Id. at 2002 (Stevens, J., dissenting).

CHAPTER 4

Fifth Amendment Protections:
Where Went *Miranda*?

THE FIFTH AMENDMENT of the United States Constitution guarantees that no person shall be compelled to incriminate one's self.[1] Accordingly, the government cannot, like many totalitarian governments, force a defendant to confess his crimes. As Justice Frankfurter stated in one of his last opinions:

> Our decisions under [the Fourteenth Amendment] have made clear that convictions following the admission into evidence of [involuntary confessions] cannot stand . . . not so much because such confessions are unlikely to be true but because the methods used to extract them offend any underlying principle in the enforcement of our criminal law: that ours is an accusatorial and not an inquisitorial system.[2]

Of course, notwithstanding Frankfurter's statement, it must be recognized that if the government was empowered to coerce confessions, it is not a very far step to be able to force an accused to say exactly what one wants to hear.[3] In any event, where a confession or admission made by an accused was not voluntarily given, the Court has ruled it inadmissible.[4]

During the height of the Warren Court, the United States Supreme Court ruled in *Escobedo v. Illinois*[5] that a defendant had a right to consult with counsel whenever he was interrogated by the police, assuming he was the focus of alleged criminality.[6] Here, the Court interjected the Sixth Amendment right to counsel into the context of police interrogation to assure that a defendant's Fifth Amendment rights were respected.[7]

In 1966, the United States Supreme Court put some teeth into the Fifth Amendment protection in its decision of *Miranda v. Arizona*.[8] In an effort to assure equal justice to indigent defendants and to guarantee police respect for the privilege against self-incrimination, the Warren Court made a bold step forward.[9] It clarified that the *Escobedo* protection extended to indigent defendants. More importantly, it created a mechanism designed to insure that a defendant's statements to the police be given voluntarily, and with an understanding of his rights during police interrogation, as well as the consequences of not asserting those rights. The Court stated:

> The prosecution may not use statements, whether exculpatory or inculpatory, stemming from custodial interrogation of the defendant unless it demonstrates the use of procedural safeguards effective to secure the privilege against self-incrimination. By custodial interrogation, we mean questioning initiated by law enforcement officers after a person has been taken into custody or otherwise deprived of his freedom of action in any significant way. As for the procedural safeguards to be employed, unless other fully effective means are devised to inform accused persons of their right of silence and to assure a continuous opportunity to exercise it, the following measures are required. Prior to any questioning, the person must be warned that he has a right to remain silent, that any statement he does make may be used as evidence against him, and that he has a right to the presence of an attorney, either retained or appointed. The defendant may waive effectuation of these rights, provided the waiver is made voluntarily, knowingly and intelligently. If, however, he indicates in any manner and at any stage of the process that he wishes to consult with an attorney before speaking there can be no questioning. Likewise, if the individual is alone and indicates in any manner that he does not wish to be interrogated, the police may not question him. The mere fact that he may have answered some questions or volunteered some statements on his own does not deprive him of the right to refrain from answering any further inquiries until he has consulted with an attorney and thereafter consents to be questioned.[10]

While severe criticism was directed at *Miranda*,[11] similar to earlier criticisms of the Fifth Amendment privilege itself,[12] the reality is that the *Miranda* admonitions have had no appreciable effect on the government's ability to extract statements from criminal suspects.[13] While some might seize upon this point by asserting that the *Miranda* protections have not achieved their purpose, such is beyond the point. What *Miranda* assures is that Fifth Amendment waivers truly are *intelligent*. It is incongruous that constitutional protections, and the consequences of waiver of those protections, might be hidden behind some veil of secrecy or, at least, mired in any abyss of confusion. Common sense dictates that not everyone—particularly the uneducated, the mentally weak, the young, and those from foreign soils who only have recently been blessed with American citizenship— may have a full understanding of their fundamental rights. The

Miranda litany is designed to assure the rights of citizens who are faced with police inquiry are not shrouded in mystery.

In any event, the Burger and Rehnquist Courts have more recently reflected a degree of apparent discomfort with the principles of *Miranda*, for the great majority of the opinions interpreting *Miranda* decided since the Warren Court period have not vigorously followed its lead. The first attacks on the *Miranda* protections came in the so-called impeachment cases of *Harris v. New York*[14] and *Oregon v. Hass*.[15] In the first case, the Court ruled in 1971 that statements taken from a suspect that had been preceded by defective warnings could be used by the government at trial to impeach the defendant's credibility.[16] In the second opinion, the Court in 1975 held that even though a defendant had exercised his *Miranda* protections, the police refusal to allow him to talk to a lawyer and their subsequent extraction of incriminating statements from him did not preclude the government from using the illegal statements to impeach his trial testimony.[17]

In 1974, the Court ruled in *Michigan v. Tucker*[18] that the *Miranda* warnings were "not themselves rights protected by the Constitution" but rather only "prophylactic standards" created to protect the integrity of the privilege against self-incrimination.[19] In that case, the defendant had been interrogated before *Miranda* had been decided.[20] He had not been fully informed of his rights prior to police questioning.[21] As a consequence of the interrogation, a witness was found who eventually testified against the defendant at a trial conducted after *Miranda* was decided.[22] The trial court excluded the defendant's statement but did allow the witness to testify at the trial.[23] Here, the Court ruled the interrogation had not deprived the defendant of his privilege against compulsory incrimination since there was no indication his statements were involuntary.[24] Rather, there had been a mere failure to make available to the defendant "the full measure of procedural safeguards associated with that right since *Miranda*."[25] Thus, the derivative use of witness testimony that was discovered through non-compliance with *Miranda* was proper. While the precedential value of *Tucker* appeared to be unclear since the *Tucker* interrogation preceded the *Miranda* decision, the Court's characterization of the *Miranda* provisions as mere prophylactic devices not necessarily mandated by the Constitution provided the Court with a mechanism for one day asserting that *Miranda* violations do not implicate *constitutional* violations and, accordingly, should not be subject to the exclusionary rule.

In 1975, the Court ruled in *Michigan v. Mosley*[26] where a defendant asserted his *Miranda* right to remain silent when questioned about one charge, this did not disallow the same police department from interrogating him later about an unrelated, second charge while he

remained in custody on the first charge.[27] Here, the Court reasoned
to hold otherwise would mean once a defendant had exercised his
right to remain silent as to one particular matter, the government
would be powerless to talk to him about any other matters he might
in fact care to discuss.[28]

In 1976, in *United States v. Mandujano*,[29] the Court determined
a person called before a grand jury did not have to receive *Miranda*
admonitions.[30] *Mandujano* might be defensible to some extent in that
Miranda requires advice about the right to counsel, which generally
has been rejected in the context of a grand jury inquiry,[31] as well as
information about the Fifth Amendment privilege, which right must
be respected in a grand jury setting. However, the Court ruled a year
later in *United States v. Wong*[32] that statements taken from a grand
jury witness could be used against her notwithstanding the absence
of an effective warning about the Fifth Amendment privilege.[33]

In 1976, the United States Supreme Court in *Beckwith v. United
States*[34] also set the groundwork for a series of decisions that have
held *Miranda* has no application unless the defendant is in "custody."[35]
In *Beckwith*, it was determined that an I.R.S. agent's questioning of
a person who was the focus of a tax fraud investigation did not
implicate *Miranda* since the person was situated in his home free of
any constraints.[36] In *Oregon v. Mathiason*,[37] decided one year later,
the Court held *Miranda* had no application where a defendant
"voluntarily" came to the police station to be questioned following a
police "request" to do so.[38]

Based on this reasoning, the Court later ruled in *California v.
Beheler*[39] that where a defendant went to the police station in the
company of the police, there was no *custodial* interrogation since they
claimed he "voluntarily agreed" to do so.[40] In *Minnesota v. Murphy*,[41]
it was held a probationer was not faced with custodial interrogation
for purposes of *Miranda* when he reported to his probation officer as
required by the terms of his probation, which included being truthful
in all matters in such meetings.[42] Most troublesome on this point was
Berkemer v. McCarty,[43] which held where a person was stopped by
police in a routine traffic stop and, subsequently, was asked whether
he was under the influence of intoxicants, to which he responded he
had drank two beers and smoked marijuana a short time before, he
was not in "custody" for *Miranda* purposes, even though the Court
conceded he was in custody for Fourth Amendment purposes.[44]

In the 1979 decision of *North Carolina v. Butler*,[45] the Court ruled
a specific written waiver of the *Miranda* protections is not required.[46]
In that case, the defendant told the police he understood his rights,
but he refused to sign a waiver form before he made an incriminating
statement.[47]

In *Fare v. Michael C.*,[48] also decided in 1979, the Court ruled where a juvenile, following *Miranda* warnings, asked to be accompanied by his probation officer, this was not an invocation of *Miranda*.[49] The Court simply reasoned *Miranda* was designed to assure the availability of a lawyer, not others, during police interrogation.[50] Even though it is common for a naive minor faced with police interrogation to wish to turn to a parent, guardian, teacher, friend, or other non-lawyer protector for advice, the Court was not sympathetic to such a person in this predicament.

Notwithstanding these various decisions, the Court did not avail itself of every opportunity to cut back on the reach of *Miranda* in the 1970s. For example, in B*rown v. Illinois*,[51] the Court ruled in 1975 that statements following an illegal arrest were not *per se* purged of the taint of the illegal arrest by intervening *Miranda* warnings.[52] The *Brown* holding was reaffirmed in two later Supreme Court decisions.[53] In addition, in *Doyle v. Ohio*,[54] the Court held in 1976 that a defendant's post-arrest silence, following *Miranda* warnings, could not be used by the state at the defendant's trial to impeach his defense testimony claim first offered at trial that he had been "framed" by the police.[55] Here, the Court thought it fundamentally unfair to advise a defendant of his right of silence and, thereafter, use that silence to attack his defense at trial.[56]

In the early 1980s, M*iranda* enjoyed some degree of resurgence. First, the Court decided in 1980 the important case of *Rhode Island v. Innis*.[57] In that case, the Court ruled in *dicta* that where a defendant is faced with the "functional equivalent" of interrogations, which arises where the police "words or actions . . . are reasonably likely to elicit an incriminating response from the suspect," *Miranda* is implicated.[58] Thus, the *dicta* suggested if the police made an affirmative statement, rather than an utterance in the form of a question,[59] or took certain action, such as displaying proceeds of a crime before a defendant, with the obvious intention of eliciting an incriminating statement, *Miranda* should apply. However, the value of this decision was minimized given the Court's refusal to find the "functional equivalent" of interrogation in the case before it.

In *Innis*, the defendant was arrested for robbery and murder shortly after the shotgun slaying of a taxicab driver.[60] When the defendant was arrested, he was unarmed.[61] After being given *Miranda* warnings, he indicated he wished to speak with a lawyer.[62] Enroute in a squad car to the police station, one officer expressed to another officer in the presence of the defendant his concern about the whereabouts of the shotgun and that there was a school for handicapped children in the vicinity where both the crime had occurred and the defendant was arrested. The officer added, "God forbid one of them might find a weapon with shells and they might hurt themselves."[63] The second officer then echoed his concern about the importance of finding the gun.[64] At this point, the defendant interrupted the officers and stated he would show them where he hid the gun and, subsequently, led them to the gun.[65] Here, the Court said there was no indication the exchange between the officers was designed to elicit, or reasonably likely to result in, an incriminating statement and, thus, no breach of *Miranda* had occurred.[66]

Furthermore, the Court's narrow view of what constitutes the functional equivalent of interrogation was fortified in *Arizona v. Mauro*.[67] In that case, police surveillance of the defendant's conversation with his wife did not constitute interrogation in circumstances where he invoked *Miranda*, whereupon police questioning ceased, but thereafter the police recorded the defendant's conversations with his wife with a tape recorder in plain sight while she desperately tried to talk to her husband about his killing of their son.[68] The Court refused to view the arrangement as a psychological ploy that could be treated as the functional equivalent of interrogation. According to the Court, the mere "possibility" this arrangement would yield incriminating evidence was insufficient to find a *Miranda* violation.[69]

Even though the Court in *Innis* and *Mauro* has not given a broad interpretation as to what constitutes the functional equivalent of interrogation, it is nonetheless significant that it has indicated interrogation is not limited to police utterances in the form of a question. Prior to *Innis*, many lower courts had adopted exactly that view. For instance, where a police officer said he wanted to show, and did display to, the defendant a damning ballistics report, which prompted a confession to a homicide, the Kentucky Supreme Court held there was no interrogation.[70] Similarly, where a police officer accused a defendant of a robbery, to which he responded with an incriminating statement, a federal district court held there was "no interrogation . . . but an accusation which elicited a spontaneous non-responsive admission . . . ."[71]

In any event, in 1981 the Court decided another important case that reaffirmed the principles of *Miranda*. In *Edwards v. Arizona*,[72] the Court distinguished *Mosley*[73] and ruled that where a suspect following the warnings requests counsel (as opposed to invoking his right to silence), the police cannot "try again" until counsel is made available "unless [he] himself initiates further communications, exchanges or conversations with the police."[74] In that case, the defendant stated he wished to talk with an attorney before discussing a homicide charge, was then placed in a cell, and, thereafter, was instructed by a jail guard that "he had" to talk to two detectives who wanted to discuss this matter further.[75] His subsequent incriminating statements to the detectives were ruled inadmissible.[76]

Later, in *Smith v. Illinois*,[77] the Court clarified the *Edwards* ruling by holding that where the defendant expressed his desire for counsel, his subsequent responses to further police questioning could not be used to cast doubt on whether he actually had exercised his right to counsel.[78] In *Smith*, the defendant responded to a police question as to whether he understood his right to counsel by answering "Uh, yeah, I'd like to do that."[79] The state court held the defendant's incriminating statements that followed demonstrated he had not clearly invoked his right to counsel.[80] The United States Supreme Court stated the defendant's initial request for counsel was explicit and unequivocal and that further questioning was not permissible.[81]

In *Oregon v. Bradshaw*,[82] the Court distinguished *Edwards* in a case where the defendant initially exercised his right to counsel, which exercise was respected by the police, and, thereafter, the *defendant* initiated a further dialogue with the police without counsel.[83] Since the defendant rather than the government had initiated the exchange, his later cooperation with the police was viewed as a waiver of counsel.[84]

The principles of *Edwards* were reinforced in the 1988 case of *Arizona v. Roberson*,[85] where the defendant asserted his right to counsel during police interrogation on one charge and, thereafter, he was interrogated about a second crime.[86] The court distinguished *Michigan v. Mosely*[87] by stating "as *Mosley* made clear, a suspect's decision to cut off questioning, unlike his request for counsel, does not raise the presumption that he is not able to proceed without a lawyer's advice."[88] The Court held a fresh set of *Miranda* warnings preceding interrogation on the second charge did not undermine the requirement that once the defendant requested counsel, no further police-initiated interrogation could occur.[89]

However, in another 1988 case, *Patterson v. Illinois*,[90] the Court clarified that the *Edwards* principle regarding counsel will not have operational effect, even as to *formally charged* defendants, until the defendant requests counsel.[91] In that case, the defendant was informed by police that he had been indicted for murder, was given *Miranda* warnings, and, thereafter, he agreed to make inculpatory statements without counsel.[92] The Court rejected the defendant's argument that, since his right to counsel attached at the point of the indictment, any subsequent police-initiated interrogation was improper.[93] In other words, until and unless a defendant demands counsel, the police can proceed.

In conclusion, the *dicta* of *Rhode Island v. Innis*[94] as well as *Edwards v. Arizona*[95] and its progeny[96] actually represented a strengthening of the principles behind *Miranda*. In a sense, these two cases in the early 1980s might have been viewed as an indication that the Burger Court was not unduly uncomfortable with *Miranda*. Another 1981 case, *Estelle v. Smith*,[97] pointed in the same direction. In that case, the Court held that a court-ordered psychiatric examination of an accused amounted to custodial interrogation and, accordingly, the psychiatrist's testimony was inadmissible since no warnings had been given.[98] However, the Court's temporary honeymoon with *Miranda* was soon to end.

Soon after *Edwards*, the Court decided *California v. Prysock*.[99] In that 1981 case, a police officer told a juvenile suspect he had the right to consult with an attorney before and during police interrogation, and, in addition, that he had the right to appointed counsel.[100] However, the officer did not explicitly advise the juvenile that he had the right to *appointed* counsel *prior* to the interrogation.[101] The state court ruled the admonition was ambiguous as it pertained to the availability of cost-free counsel prior to and during the interrogation.[102] The Supreme Court summarily reversed the state court, while proclaiming no "talismanic incantation" of *Miranda* warnings were required,[103] even though the dissent pointed out:

> Because lawyers are normally "appointed" by judges, and not by law enforcement officers, the reference to appointed counsel could reasonably have been understood to refer to *trial* counsel.[104]

In *Wyrick v. Fields*,[105] the Supreme Court in 1982 addressed the scope of an earlier *Miranda* waiver as it might affect subsequent stages of an interrogation. Here, a defendant agreed to a polygraph examination after making a complete waiver of his *Miranda* protections.[106] After the polygraph examination had been completed, the examiner indicated he had concluded that the defendant had been deceitful in his answers and asked him if he could explain why his answers were bothering him.[107] At this point, the defendant made incriminating admissions.[108] A federal court ruled that the *Miranda* waiver only covered the polygraph examination and not the subsequent questions about the unfavorable test results.[109] However, the Supreme Court disagreed and held once a valid waiver had occurred, it was operable in subsequent stages of the interrogation process and, accordingly, the defendant did not have to be readvised of his rights prior to the follow-up questions.[110] *Wyrick*, then, could be read to hold that where a multiple-stage interrogation process occurs, the warnings need only be given at the commencement of the process rather than at the beginning of each individual stage.

However, the *Prysock* and *Wyrick* rulings paled by comparison to what followed in two major cases. First came the decision of *New York v. Quarles*[111] in 1984. In that case, a woman reported to police that she had just been raped and that the rapist had entered a supermarket armed with a gun.[112] After the police entered the store, the defendant ran through the establishment attempting to evade police capture but was apprehended.[113] Upon searching the defendant, they found an empty shoulder holster on his person and asked him where the gun was.[114] He responded, while nodding in the direction of certain empty cartons, "The gun is over there."[115] The state courts suppressed the defendant's response as well as the gun since the police question about the whereabouts of the gun had not been preceded by *Miranda* warnings.[116] The Supreme Court held that the "overriding considerations of public safety justify the officer's failure to provide *Miranda* warnings before he asked questions devoted to locating the abandoned weapon."[117] Justice O'Connor, who usually sides with the contingent on the Court that limits the reach of *Miranda*, wrote a separate opinion.[118]

> In my view, a "public safety" exception unnecessarily blurs the edges of the clear line heretofore established and makes *Miranda's* requirements more difficult to understand. * * * The end result will be a finespun new doctrine on public safety exigencies incident to custodial interrogation, complete with hair-splitting distinctions that currently plague our Fourth Amendment jurisprudence.[119]

Meanwhile, the dissent wondered out loud as to whose safety was threatened.[120] When the question was asked of the defendant, he already had been handcuffed and was surrounded by four officers, who had returned their own guns to their holsters because, as one officer later testified, the situation was under control.[121] Furthermore, the entire incident occurred at 12:30 A.M. while the supermarket was apparently abandoned except for clerks at the checkout counter.[122] Thus, the police could have easily cordoned off the store and searched it for the missing gun.[123] In the final analysis, the dissent was bewildered as to how the majority could find a threat to public safety when the New York courts had determined as a factual matter that none existed.[124]

An even more powerful blow was inflicted on *Miranda* in 1985 in *Oregon v. Elstad*.[125] In that case, police conducted an arrest of the defendant in his home pursuant to a warrant.[126] Before he was told about the warrant authorizing his arrest for a burglary, one of the arresting officers stated he "felt" the defendant had been involved in the burglary in question and the defendant responded, "Yes, I was there."[127] After the defendant was taken to police headquarters, he was given *Miranda* warnings for the first time.[128] Immediately thereafter, the defendant confirmed his involvement in the burglary and signed a typed confession.[129] The state court of appeals ruled the written confession was tainted by the earlier *Miranda* violation in the defendant's home since the "cat was sufficiently out of the bag to exert a coercive impact on . . . the later confession."[130] But the Untied States Supreme Court saw the matter differently:

> The *Miranda* exclusionary rule [unlike the Fourth Amendment exclusionary rule] . . . serves the Fifth Amendment and sweeps more broadly than the Fifth Amendment itself. It may be triggered even in the absence of a Fifth Amendment violation. The Fifth Amendment prohibits use by the prosecution in its case in chief only of *compelled* testimony. Failure to administer *Miranda* creates a presumption of compulsion.[131]

Thus, while the government might not be able to use the earlier admission not preceded by the warning because of the presumption of coercion that attaches to it, it could use the later confession if demonstrated it was not coerced.[132]

> We believe that this reasoning applied with equal force when alleged "fruit" of a noncoercive *Miranda* violation is neither a witness nor an article of evidence but the accused's own voluntary testimony.[133]

The Court also distinguished the "voluntariness" cases.

> There is a vast difference between the direct consequences flowing from coercion of a confession by physical violence or other deliberate means calculated to break the suspect's will and the uncertain consequences of disclosure of a "guilty secret" freely given in response to an unwarned but noncoercive question, as in this case.[134]

Here, the dictates of *Miranda* were served by suppressing the unwarned statement and not the subsequent confession.[135] By resurrecting the *Michigan v. Tucker*[136] proposition that *Miranda* protections afford protections broader than those accorded suspects by the Fifth Amendment, the Court effectively minimized the importance of *Miranda* warnings.

Elstadt is exceedingly important, then, for two reasons. First, by asserting a non-warned statement does not taint a subsequently warned statement that may be an immediate by-product of the first statement, the Court has created a mechanism where police can easily circumvent *Miranda*. Simply put: interrogate the defendant without reference to the *Miranda* litany, extract an incriminating statement, and now, "with the cat out of the bag," instruct him pursuant to *Miranda* and have him repeat what he has already reported. Second, and most troublesome, if unwarned statements are at best only *presumed* coercive, why could the state not rebut the presumption with evidence that the *initial* statement, albeit unwarned, was not coerced? Of course, if the initial statement was not coerced, it too might be admissible. Clearly, *Elstad* and its predecessor *Tucker* have laid the groundwork for a future Court ruling that determines non-compliance with *Miranda* does not necessarily mean that incriminating statements that immediately follow must be suppressed.

In 1986, the Court limited the reach of *Miranda* in two more significant cases. In *Morgan v. Burbine*,[137] a defendant challenged his otherwise voluntary confession because (1) the police failed to disclose to him the fact that a public defender was attempting to contact him and (2) that police had deceived the attorney about their intentions in continuing to interrogate him.[138] The Court ruled that *Miranda* did not require the police to notify the defendant about the attorney's interest in providing him counsel during the interrogation nor create a rule as to how the police must treat counsel.[139]

In another 1986 case, *Colorado v. Connelly*,[140] a confession taken from a mentally unfit defendant was found admissible.[141] The Court refused to hold that the defendant's mental difficulties precluded an effective waiver of the *Miranda* protections or otherwise rendered his confession involuntary.[142]

However, 1986 did not go by without some success for the defenders of *Miranda*. In *Wainwright v. Greenfield*,[143] the Court extended the principles of *Doyle v. Ohio*[144] when it held a defendant's post-*Miranda* warnings silence and request for counsel could not be used as substantive evidence to rebut his defense of insanity.[145] In addition, in *Michigan v. Jackson*,[146] the Court reinforced the doctrine behind *Edwards v. Arizona*[147] when it ruled a defendant's assertion of his right to counsel "at an arraignment or similar type of hearing" could not be followed by police-initiated interrogation.[148] However, the Court also stated in *Jackson* that interrogation could proceed if the defendant initiated further contact with the police.[149]

In 1987, the Court decided several *Miranda* decisions, none of which accepted the respective defendants' petitions for relief. Beyond *Arizona v. Mauro*,[150] where the Court rejected the defendant's argument that police taping of his conversation with his wife, who insisted on talking about the defendant's killing of their son, constituted the functional equivalent of interrogation,[151] the Court decided three other cases. First, in *Connecticut v. Barrett*,[152] the Court indicated the right to counsel under *Miranda* could be the subject of a conditional waiver.[153] The defendant had stated that he was unwilling to make a written statement unless an attorney was present but did not agree to talk to the police orally without counsel.[154] The Court concluded that although the defendant had demanded an attorney, his exercise of the right to counsel only prohibited the police from taking a written statement without counsel and did not bar their taking an oral statement form him.[155] By reason of *Barrett*, which introduces in the *Miranda* jurisprudence a concept of *partial* waiver of counsel, police can now subvert the *Edwards* principle, which says police-initiated interrogation cannot follow request for counsel, by simply asking a defendant at the outset if he wishes to make a *written* statement without an attorney. Even if he refuses, police can press on with further questioning in the hopes of gaining an oral confession.

The next case, *Colorado v. Spring*,[156] held a defendant need not be informed about the subject matter that is the focus of police questioning.[157] In that case, the defendant was arrested for firearms violations.[158] After his arrest and his waiver of *Miranda* rights, the police gradually moved to general questions about his criminal record and, thereafter, to his possible involvement in a murder.[159] At this point, the defendant admitted "I shot another guy once," but more specific questions about the killing were met with denials.[160] Two months later, the defendant was interrogated again about the murder and he confessed.[161] The state court ruled that the police were required to admonish him about the subject matter behind their initial interrogation, and their failure to do so tainted the later confession.[162] However, the United States Supreme Court held a defendant's lack of knowledge about the subject matter did not negate a "knowing and intelligent" waiver of the *Miranda* protections.[163] Moreover, the majority disagreed with the dissent[164] that the situation involved police "trickery" that invalidated the waiver.[165] In any event, by tolerating some degree of deceit by police, the *Spring* ruling opens the door to police dialogue with a defendant where they suggest that their only concern is gaining information about a minor transgression in which the defendant was involved, when in reality the true focus of their exchange with the accused is another more significant matter.

Finally, in 1987, the Court decided Bu*chanan v. Kentucky*,[166] which although was not an opinion that involved *Miranda per se*, it did undermine the reach of an earlier *Miranda* decision. In *Buchanan*, the Court limited *Estelle v. Smith*,[167] which held that a court-ordered psychiatric examination of a defendant constituted interrogation for *Miranda* purposes,[168] to its specific facts.[169] The Court ruled in *Buchanan* that when a defendant asserts the insanity defense, introduces supporting psychiatric testimony, or requests a psychiatric examination, he has no Fifth Amendment privilege against the introduction of the psychiatric testimony by the prosecution.[170] Here, the Court indicated the introduction of a psychiatrist's report regarding the accused's mental state for rebuttal purposes involved no Fifth Amendment violation when all of the defendant's statements dealing with the offenses charged were omitted.[171]

After the earlier discussed 1988 cases of *Arizona v. Roberson*,[172] which expanded the *Edwards* principle,[173] and *Patterson v. Illinois*,[174] which limited *Edwards*,[175] the Court decided *Pennsylvania v. Bruder*.[176] In *Bruder*, the Court echoed its earlier holding of *Berkemer v. McCarty*,[177] where it ruled that when police, following a traffic stop, asked the defendant several questions and requested that he perform a balancing test to determine his sobriety, this was not a "custody" situation to be preceded by *Miranda* warnings.[178]

An important 1989 decision, *Duckworth v. Eagan*,[179] approved a *Miranda* admonition that could be quite misleading to suspects. In that case, the police read to the defendant a *Miranda* waiver form and then asked him to sign it.[180] It contained the usual statements regarding the right to remain silent and the right to the presence of an attorney during interrogation, but it added: "We have no way of giving you a lawyer, but one will be appointed for you, if you wish, *if and when you go to court.*"[181] Later, the defendant confessed to a murder and was convicted.[182] The United States Court of Appeals for the Seventh Circuit reversed the defendant's conviction because it felt the warning did not provide the accused with a clear and unequivocal warning regarding the right to appointed counsel before interrogation and linked an indigent's right to counsel before interrogation with a future event.[183] However, the Supreme Court reversed in a 5–4 opinion and held the warning was consistent with *Miranda*.[184] The Court stated *Miranda* did "not require that attorneys be producible on call," only that the indigent defendant be informed of his right to the presence of appointed counsel before and during questioning and held the "if and when you go to court" qualification was consistent with the common practice of not assigning appointed counsel until the defendant's initial court appearance.[185] Be that as it may, however, the admonitions in the waiver form approved by the Court in *Duckworth*, which one can anticipate will be adopted in many police agencies, could be interpreted by an indigent suspect as an indication that the Constitution does *not* guarantee appointed counsel in the police interrogation setting until after that point where a charge is formalized against him in a court of law.[186]

In 1990, the Court decided *Illinois v. Perkins*,[187] wherein it ruled an undercover police officer posing as a fellow inmate was not required to give *Miranda* warnings to an incarcerated suspect before asking him questions that elicited an incriminating response.[188] Here, the Court reasoned the *Miranda* warnings were designed to preserve a suspect's privilege against interrogation in the context of a "police-dominated atmosphere" where "compulsion" was a real possibility.[189] In this setting where the suspect had no reason to believe that the undercover police officer in his cell block was in fact a member of the law enforcement establishment, the Court could not surmise how any coercive police forces could have influenced the suspect's willingness to make an incriminating statement.[190] The dissent pointed out, to no avail, that the plain terms of *Miranda* mandated the warnings anytime a person is faced with "custodial interrogation," which was the case here.[191]

Another case decided that term was *Pennsylvania v. Muniz*,[192] where the Court analyzed the reach of the *Miranda* doctrine in the situation where the police are videotaping responses and comments uttered by a drunk driving arrestee while he was being booked and tested for sobriety.[193] Without being given *Miranda* warnings, the defendant was asked seven questions regarding his name, address, height, weight, eye color, date of birth, and current age, during which time he verbally stumbled in his responses.[194] The defendant was asked the date of his sixth birthday, which he was unable to answer.[195] Finally, he made several incriminating statements during the course of the sobriety testing.[196] Both the audio and visual portions of the videotape recording were admitted into evidence at his trial over his objection, and he was convicted.[197] The *Muniz* Court evaluated each of the defendant's responses from the standpoint of whether they implicated the "testimonial" or "compulsion" components of the privilege against self-incrimination.[198] First, they determined the slurred nature of defendant's speech, which manifested itself during his responses to several of the questions, did not involve testimonial concerns protected by the Fifth Amendment.[199] Next, they found that his responses to the questions about the date of his sixth birthday was testimonial because the content of his answer supported an inference of mental confusion and, hence, was inadmissible.[200] Additionally, the Court ruled the seven questions were non-testimonial and admissible since they merely involved biographical data necessary to complete the booking process.[201] Finally, they determined the defendant's statements made during the sobriety testing had been volunteered and had not been made in response to custodial interrogation.[202]

In *Minick v. Mississippi*,[203] the Court interpreted the *Edwards* doctrine[204] to preclude the reinitiating the questioning of a defendant without his attorney present after he had invoked his *Miranda* right to consult with counsel *and* had in fact consulted with his attorney.[205] Here, the government had unsuccessfully argued that once a defendant had the opportunity actually to consult with his lawyer, this suspended or terminated the *Edwards* protection against further police-initiated questioning without counsel.[206]

In *McNeil v. Wisconsin*,[207] the Court narrowed the reach of *Michigan v. Jackson*[208] and *Arizona v. Roberson*.[209] In that case, the defendant appeared with counsel at his initial court appearance on an armed robbery charge.[210] Later, while still in custody, police officers approached the defendant about several separate uncharged crimes including murder.[211] After providing the defendant with *Miranda* warnings regarding the latter crimes, defendant agreed to talk. Eeventually, he made incriminating statements about these offenses.[212] After unsuccessfully moving to suppress the incriminating statements, the defendant was convicted of these charges and appealed.[213]

The defendant argued that when he made his initial court appearance on the earlier unrelated armed robbery charge represented by counsel, this amounted to an invocation of his Sixth Amendment right to counsel precluding police-initiated interrogation on *any* charge.[214] However, the Court ruled the Sixth Amendment right to counsel is "offense-specific" and the *Jackson* bar against police interrogation is similarly offense-specific to the charged offense and not the unrelated, uncharged offense.[215]

In a dizzying display of dancing around precedent, principle, and common sense policy, Justice Scalia demonstrated his keen ability to split hairs in a thinly disguised effort to immerse the jurisprudence of *Miranda* into the mire of total confusion. Writing for the Court, he said an exercise of the Sixth Amendment right to counsel is "different" than an exercise of the "Fifth Amendment" right to counsel protected by *Miranda*, *Edwards*, and *Roberson*, which is not offense-specific.[216] The opinion indicated the Sixth Amendment right does not attach until a prosecution has "commenced" and thus cannot be invoked for uncharged crimes.[217] In contrast, the Fifth Amendment right is designed to protect one faced with the "inherently compelling pressures" of custodial interrogation, which, when invoked, attaches to all crimes, charged or uncharged.[218] The "purpose" of the Sixth Amendment right, said Justice Scalia at his rhetorical best, is to protect the "unaided layman" only *after* the "adverse position of government and defendant had solidified" by reason of the formal charge.[219] The "purpose" of the Fifth Amendment right, said the Court, was to protect a "quite different interest," namely, the suspect's "desire to deal with the police through counsel."[220] An exercise of the Sixth Amendment right, said His Honor, does not require an "expression" by the accused that he wishes to deal with the authorities through counsel in future encounters since such is "presumed" under the Sixth Amendment by his *action* in appearing with counsel at his first court appearance.[221] An exercise of the Fifth Amendment right, apparently not carrying such a presumption, requires such an *express request* for counsel.[222] Here, when defendant had made his incriminating statements on the later charges, he had only exercised his Sixth Amendment "offense-specific" right to counsel on the earlier named charge and he had *not* "expressly" exercised his

Fifth Amendment right on the latter uncharged crimes.[223] To rule
that an exercise of the Sixth Amendment right to counsel should not
be "offense-specific," the opinion predictably concludes, would be to
fashion a rule that would "seriously impede effective law
enforcement."[224]

In dissent, Justice Stevens condemned the majority ruling for
being "symbolic" of a "preference for an inquisitorial system that
regards the defense lawyer as an impediment rather than a servant
to the cause of justice."[225] He stated placement of an "offense-specific"
limitation on the Sixth Amendment was at odds with prior decisions
that deliberately gave an expansive rather than a narrow interpretation
to a defendant's exercise of his right to counsel.[226] He criticized the
ruling for not taking into account the "common sense reality" that
many suspects will not understand *which* right to counsel they are
invoking or *how* to best protect their constitutional interests.[227] Next,
it interferes with the "substance of the attorney-client relationship"
which contemplates a client's dependence on counsel in a wide range
of subject matters not divisible into so many segments.[228] Also, the
majority ruling can only "generate confusion in the law."[229] Finally,
Justice Stevens suggested the majority ruling is possibly best explained
by the majority's "fear" that counsel may impede law enforcement.[230]

The *McNeil* Court reliance on crime control as a legitimate reason
to interpret the Sixth Amendment right to counsel as being offense-
specific is an excellent example of the King without his clothes. None
of Justice Scalia's semantics hide the obvious: it is appropriate to
have some "due process" but inappropriate to have it "seriously impede"
crime control; it is appropriate to have some suspects exercise their
rights some of the time but inappropriate to have it "seriously impede
law enforcement."

While some commentators continue to criticize[231] and others
defend[232] *Miranda*, the comments of Professor Ronald Collins in a
popular legal periodical[233] may be most apt in this connection. He
found in 1989 that "[s]ince 1971, the Court had rendered opinions
in some 30 notable Fifth Amendment *Miranda* cases. In only five
(three of them involving the same point of law) did *Miranda's* promise
rescue the person claiming the constitutional right."[234] But, more to
the point, he noted:

> What *Miranda's* defenders do not realize is that *Miranda's* critics
> depend on its symbolic survival. How could they publicly endorse
> abandoning this uniquely American symbol of justice? [Critics on the
> Court] would no more overrule it than they would curse *Marbury
> v. Madison*—the very symbol of their own power.

Miranda's critics have the best of both worlds. On the one hand, if they bow in word to the precedent, then the ideal of justice appears reserved. On the other hand, if they take action to dismember *Miranda*, then street justice prevails over constitutional justice. Preserving the *Miranda* symbol leaves the public impression that the rule is taking the police hostage at a time when society is besieged by crime. For although the public too pays homage to the symbol, today it feeds first on the fear of crime.

This dualism is a blessing for *Miranda's* critics. That is, constitutional cutbacks are justified in the name of public calls for punitive action. In this Sisyphean sense, *Miranda's* very existence serves to justify its demise. But without the *Miranda* camouflage, the cutbacks would be seen for what they are—a too often foreign, and therefore un-American, brand of justice molded increasingly to serve a police-favored state.[235]

Thus, *Miranda* protections, like the exclusionary rule and Fourth Amendment protections, probably will not be abruptly abolished by the Court. They will be maintained to *some* degree as an expression of our sense of fairness in dealing with a suspect who faces the accusatorial powers of the government. Each time the ordinary citizen hears a police officer rattle off the *Miranda* warnings to a suspect in a popular television series, he will be reminded that there exists some barriers between the potential innocent and potential overzealous police. Each time the constitutional scholar reads the next in a series of *Miranda* decisions that cuts a piece out of the *Miranda* apple, he may take solace in the fact that some portion of the apple core remains in tact. And, of course, the nourishment provided by the continual whittling away of *Miranda*, reflected in case law limiting its scope, will serve to feed the need to assure us that no criminal should go free as a result of some "technicality." And, finally, as the apple continues to lose its shine, the interminable debate will continue over whether the apple is merely ripe or whether it is rotten to the core.

NOTES

1. U.S. Const. Amend. V.
2. Rogers v. Richmond, 365 U.S. 534, 540–41 (1961).
3. *See, e.g.*, Brown v. Mississippi, 297 U.S. 278 (1936) (defendants charged with murder confessed following brutal beatings, whippings, and hanging from ropes; confession inadmissible). *See also* Mary Ann Williams, *Torture in Chicago*, 12 CHI. LAWYER 1 (No. 3, March 1989) (report on alleged police

abuse and torture of suspects in investigation of murder of two Chicago police officers).

4. *See, e.g.*, Townsend v. Sain, 372 U.S. 293 (1963) (use of drug with properties of truth serum); Lynum v. Illinois, 372 U.S. 528 (1963) (threatening defendant with taking away custody of her children); Spano v. New York, 360 U.S. 315 (1959) (psychologically coercive police methods); Brown v. Mississippi, 297 U.S. 278 (1936) (physical coercion).

5. 378 U.S. 478 (1964).

6. *Id.* at 490–91.

7. In this case, the petitioner had become the accused, and the purpose of the interrogation was to "get him" to confess his guilt despite his constitutional right not to do so. *Id.* at 485.

8. 384 U.S. 436 (1966).

9. It is clear that the Court, during this period, was sensitive about giving the Bill of Rights real meaning within the context of criminal procedure. *See* Arthur J. Goldberg, EQUAL JUSTICE: THE WARREN ERA OF THE SUPREME COURT, 3–31 (1971).

10. 384 U.S. at 444–45, 471–79.

11. *See, e.g.*, Gerald M. Chaplain, *Questioning* Miranda, 38 VAND. L. REV. 1417 (1985); Joseph D. Grano, *Prophylactic Rules in Criminal Procedure: A Question of Article III Legitimacy*, 80 NW. U.L. REV. 100 (1985); Fred Inbau, *Over-Reaction—the Mischief of* Miranda v. Arizona, 73 J. CRIM. L. & CRIMINOLOGY 797 (1982).

12. Henry J. Friendly, *The Fifth Amendment Tomorrow: The Case for Constitutional Change*, 37 U. CINN. L. REV. 671, 713–14, 721–22 (1970) (would allow trial court to make unfavorable comment to jury about defendant's refusal to be interrogated in judicially supervised interrogation).

13. *See* Special Project, *Interrogations in New Haven: The Impact of* Miranda, 76 YALE L. J. 1519 (1967); Lawrence S. Leiken, *Police Interrogation in Colorado: The Implementation of* Miranda, 47 DEN. L. J. 1 (1970).

14. 401 U.S. 222 (1971).

15. 420 U.S. 714 (1975).

16. 401 U.S. at 225–26.

17. 420 U.S. at 721–23. *See also* United States v. Havens, 446 U.S. 620 (1980).

18. 417 U.S. 433 (1974).

19. *Id.* at 444–46.

20. *Miranda* was not given complete retroactive application. In Johnson v. New Jersey, 384 U.S. 719 (1966), the Court held that *Miranda* affected only those cases in which the trial began after the decision had been rendered. *Id.* at 732,

21. 417 U.S. at 435–37.

22. *Id.* at 436–37.

23. *Id.* at 437.

24. *Id.* at 444–45.

25. *Id.* at 444.

26. 423 U.S. 96 (1975).

27. *Id.* at 104–07.

28. *Id.* at 102–03.
29. 425 U.S. 564 (1976).
30. *Id.* at 579.
31. *In re* Groban, 352 U.S. 330 (1957) (dictum); Wayne LaFave & Jerold Israel, CRIMINAL PROCEDURE, sec. 8.13(a) (1984) (lower courts uniformly interpret *Groban* as not requiring counsel).
32. 431 U.S. 174 (1977).
33. *Id.* at 177–80.
34. 425 U.S. 341 (1976).
35. *See infra* notes 37–44 and accompanying text.
36. 425 U.S. at 344.
37. 429 U.S. 492 (1977).
38. *Id.* at 495.
39. 463 U.S. 1121 (1983) (per curiam).
40. *Id.* at 1125.
41. 465 U.S. 420 (1984).
42. *Id.* at 430–34.
43. 468 U.S. 420 (1984).
44. *Id.* at 436–37.
45. 441 U.S. 369 (1979).
46. *Id.* at 373.
47. *Id.* at 371.
48. 442 U.S. 707 (1979).
49. *Id.* at 724.
50. *Id.* at 718–19.
51. 422 U.S. 590 (1975).
52. *Id.* at 600–03.
53. Taylor v. Alabama, 457 U.S. 687 (1982); Dunaway v. New York, 442 U.S. 200 (1979).
54. 426 U.S. 610 (1976).
55. *Id.* at 619. *But see* Jenkins v. Anderson, 447 U.S. 231 (1980), where the Court allowed the states to impeach the defendant's claim of self-defense first offered in a murder trial with his pre-arrest silence, where the silence had in no way been encouraged by *Miranda* warnings, and Fletcher v. Weir, 455 U.S. 603 (1982) (per curiam), where the Court permitted the state to use the defendant's post-arrest silence to impeach his defense theory first offered at trial, where his silence in no way was prompted by *Miranda* admonitions.
56. 426 U.S. at 618–19.
57. 446 U.S. 291 (1980).
58. *Id.* at 300–01.
59. *E.g.,* "Joe, we believe you committed this burglary"; or "Joe, we must tell you, we found your fingerprints on the murder weapon."
60. 446 U.S. at 293–94.
61. *Id.* at 294.
62. *Id.*
63. *Id.* at 294–95.
64. *Id.* at 295.

65. *Id.*
66. *Id.* at 302–03.
67. 481 U.S. 520 (1987).
68. *Id.* at 522–25.
69. *Id.* at 528–29.
70. Combs v. Commonwealth, 438 S.W.2d 82 (Ky. 1969).
71. United States *ex rel.* Ellington v. Conboy, 333 F. Supp. 1318 (S.D.N.Y. 1971).
72. 451 U.S. 477 (1981).
73. *Id.* at 485.
74. *Id.* at 484–85.
75. *Id.* at 478–79.
76. *Id.* at 480.
77. 469 U.S. 91 (1984).
78. *Id.* at 100.
79. *Id.* at 93.
80. *Id.* at 94.
81. *Id.* at 99–100.
82. 462 U.S. 1039 (1983) (plurality opinion).
83. *Id.* at 1045–46.
84. *Id.*
85. 486 U.S. 675 (1988).
86. *Id.* at 682.
87. *See supra* notes 26–28 and accompanying text.
88. 486 U.S. at 683.
89. *Id.*
90. 487 U.S. 285 (1988).
91. *Id.* at 291.
92. *Id.* at 288–89.
93. *Id.* at 290–91.
94. *See supra* notes 57–59 and accompanying text.
95. *See supra* notes 72–76 and accompanying text.
96. *See supra* notes 77–93 and accompanying text.
97. 451 U.S. 454 (1981).
98. *Id.* at 468–69.
99. 453 U.S. 355 (1981) (per curiam).
100. *Id.* at 356–57.
101. *Id.* at 358–59.
102. *Id.*
103. *Id.* at 359–60.
104. *Id.* at 364. (Stevens, J., dissenting) (emphasis added).
105. 459 U.S. 42 (1982).
106. *Id* at 44.
107. *Id.*
108. *Id.* at 44–45.
109. *Id.* at 45–46.
110. *Id.* at 47–49.
111. 467 U.S. 649 (1984).

112. *Id.* at 651–52.
113. *Id.* at 652.
114. *Id.*
115. *Id.*
116. *Id.* at 652–53.
117. *Id.* at 651.
118. *Id.* at 660–74 (O'Connor, J., concurring in part and dissenting in part). Justice O'Connor would have suppressed the statement but not the gun since "nothing in *Miranda* or the privilege itself requires exclusion of nontestimonial evidence derived from informal custodial interrogation." *Id.* at 660.
119. *Id.* at 663–64 (O'Connor, J., concurring in part and dissenting in part).
120. *Id.* at 675 (Marshall, J., dissenting).
121. *Id.* (Marshall, J., dissenting).
122. *Id.* at 676 (Marshall, J., dissenting).
123. *Id.* (Marshall, J., dissenting).
124. *Id.* (Marshall, J., dissenting).
125. 470 U.S. 298 (1985).
126. *Id.* at 300–01.
127. *Id.* at 301.
128. *Id.*
129. *Id.*
130. *Id.* at 302–03.
131. *Id.* at 306–07.
132. *Id.* at 307–08.
133. *Id.* at 308.
134. *Id.* at 312.
135. *Id.* at 312–14.
136. *See supra* notes 18–25 and accompanying text.
137. 475 U.S. 412 (1886).
138. *Id.* at 417–18.
139. *Id.* at 422–23.
140. 479 U.S. 157 (1986).
141. *Id.* at 167.
142. *Id.* at 170–71.
143. 474 U.S. 284 (1986).
144. *See supra* notes 54–56 and accompanying text.
145. 474 U.S. at 295.
146. 475 U.S 625 (1986).
147. *See supra* notes 72–76 and accompanying text.
148. 475 U.S. at 636.
149. *Id.* at 628.
150. 481 U.S. 520 (1987).
151. *See supra* notes 67–69 and accompanying text.
152. 479 U.S. 523 (1987).
153. *Id.* at 527–29.
154. *Id.* at 525.
155. *Id.* at 528–29.
156. 479 U.S. 564 (1987).

157. *Id.* at 575–77.
158. *Id.* at 566.
159. *Id.* at 567–68.
160. *Id.*
161. *Id.*
162. *Id.* at 568.
163. *Id.* at 576–77.
164. *Id.* at 579–81 (Marshall, J., with Brennan, J., dissenting).
165. *Id.* at 575–76.
166. 483 U.S. 402 (1987).
167. 451 U.S. 454 (1981).
168. *See supra* notes 97–98 and accompanying text.
169. 483 U.S. at 423–25.
170. *Id.* at 423–24.
171. *Id.*
172. 108 S. Ct. 2093 (1988).
173. *See supra* notes 85–89 and accompanying text.
174. 108 S.Ct. 2389 (1988).
175. *See supra* notes 90–93 and accompanying text.
176. 109 S. Ct. 205 (1988).
177. 468 U.S. 420 (1984).
178. *Id.* at 442.
179. 109 S. Ct. 2875 (1989).
180. *Id.* at 2877.
181. *Id.* (emphasis added).
182. *Id.* at 2878.
183. *Id.*
184. *Id.* at 2880.
185. *Id.*
186. *Id.* at 2886 (Marshall, J., dissenting).
187. 110 S. Ct. 2394 (1990).
188. *Id.* at 2399.
189. *Id.* at 2397.
190. *Id.* at 2397–98.
191. *Id.* at 2401–04 (Marshall, J., dissenting).
192. 110 S. Ct. 2638 (1990).
193. *See id.* at 2639.
194. *Id.*
195. *Id.*
196. *Id.*
197. *Id.*
198. *Id.* at 2643–44.
199. *Id.* at 2644–45.
200. *Id.* at 2645–49.
201. *Id.* at 2649–50.
202. *Id.* at 2650–52.
203. 111 S. Ct. 486 (1990).

204. Edwards v. Arizona, 451 U.S. 447 (1981) (police may not initiate interrogation of a suspect after he has exercised his right to counsel).
205. 111 S. Ct. at 489–92.
206. *Id.* at 489.
207. 111 S. Ct. 2204 (1991).
208. 475 U.S. 625 (1986).
209. 486 U.S. 675 (1988).
210. 111 S.Ct. at 2206.
211. *Id.*
212. *Id.* at 2206–07.
213. *Id.* at 2207.
214. *Id.*
215. *Id.* at 2207–08.
216. *Id.* at 2208.
217. *Id.* at 2207–08.
218. *Id.* at 2208.
219. *Id.* at 2208–09.
220. *Id.* at 2209.
221. *Id.* at 2209–10.
222. *Id.* at 2210.
223. *Id.* at 2207–11.
224. *Id.* at 2210.
225. *Id.* at 2212 (Stevens, J., dissenting).
226. *Id.*
227. *Id.* at 2212–13.
228. *Id.* at 2213–14.
229. *Id.* at 2214.
230. *Id.*
231. *See, e.g.*, Joseph D. Grano, *Police Interrogation and the Constitution: Doctrinal Tension and An Uncertain Future*, 25 CRIM. L. BULL. 5 (1989).
232. *See, e.g.*, Paul Marcus, *Defending* Miranda, 24 LAND & WATER L. REV. 241 (1989).
233. Ronald K.L. Collins, *Is* Miranda *Crumbling?* 11 NAT'L L. J. 15 (Feb. 20, 1989).
234. *Id.* at 18.
235. *Id.*

CHAPTER 5

Sixth Amendment Right to Counsel:
Has *Gideon*'s Trumpet Blown Away?

FEW DECISIONS of the United States Supreme Court have been more heralded than *Gideon v. Wainwright*,[1] wherein the Warren Court in 1963 overruled an earlier opinion[2] and proclaimed the right to counsel, appointed or retained, was a fundamental right at trial guaranteed by the Sixth Amendment.[3] The Court reasoned that because government entities routinely spend "vast sums of money" to prosecute criminals and that because few defendants who even have the financial means to do so "fail to hire the best lawyers they can get to prepare and present their defenses," it was evident that "lawyers in criminal courts are necessities, not luxuries."[4] Moreover, the Court stated the "noble idea" that "every defendant stands equal before the law" could not be realized without the "guiding hand of counsel *at every step in the proceeding.*"[5]

A chronicle of the *Gideon* case, *Gideon's Trumpet*,[6] eventually became a best-selling book and later became a major theater and T.V. production. The importance of this case cannot be understated. The impact of Gideon was clearly designed to assure the invidious effects of poverty would not place restrictions on the exercise of one's constitutional rights—the right to trial by jury, the right to confront one's accusers, and the like—when confronted with the forces of the criminal justice system.[7] Soon, the promise of equal justice that was at the heart of *Gideon* was extended to situations beyond the trial itself. Gideon's trumpet was blaring.

In a flurry of opinions that followed, the statement in Gideon that the guiding hand of counsel was a necessity during "every step" along the road of the criminal justice process was taken most seriously, as the Court found virtually every such step to be a "critical stage"[8] where the right to counsel was now a due process guarantee. By the early 1970s, the Court had ruled this right, which included cost-free counsel for the indigent, extended to police interrogation situations,[9] lineups,[10] preliminary examinations,[11] guilty plea proceedings,[12] trials,[13] juvenile delinquency proceedings,[14] sentencing hearings,[15] and direct appeals.[16] Furthermore, the Court ruled no person could be imprisoned for any offense, including misdemeanors, unless his or her wish to be represented by counsel was respected.[17] Finally, the Court held a judge at the trial level was required to indulge every reasonable presumption *against* an accused's alleged waiver of counsel during each critical stage of the proceedings.[18]

However, like the erosion of *Miranda* that commenced in the early 1970s, the *Gideon* progeny suffered a noticeable demise following that point where the Warren Court legacy became history and the more conservative Burger and Rehnquist Courts, respectively, assumed control over federal constitutional interpretations. The first dramatic change occurred in 1972 in *Kirby v. Illinois*.[19] Prior to *Kirby*, the Court had ruled in two 1967 companion cases that a pre-trial identification proceeding, such as a lineup or showup, was a critical stage protected by the right to counsel.[20]

In the first of these two opinions, *United States v. Wade*,[21] the Court reasoned the following potential problems were inherent in pre-trial identification situations: (1) witnesses and victims of crime often make mistaken pre-trial identifications;[22] (2) a major consideration explaining many of these misidentifications "has been the degree of suggestion inherent in the manner in which the prosecution presents the suspect" in the lineup or showup;[23] (3) after the pre-trial identification has occurred, the witness or victim "is not likely to go back on his word later on," with the result that pre-trial identification becomes more important than the identification made at trial;[24] and (4) the defense may find it difficult, if not impossible, to reconstruct after the fact the extent of prejudice the suspect suffered during the pre-trial identification.[25] Those realities in combination, said the *Wade* court, undermines the defendant's right to a *meaningful* cross-examination of the witnesses against him and to the *effective* assistance of counsel at the trial itself.[26]

> It is central to [the constitutional] principle that in addition to counsel's presence at trial, the accused is guaranteed that he need not stand alone against the State at any stage of the prosecution, formal or informal, in court or out, where counsel's absence might derogate from the accused's right to a fair trial.[27]

Here, the Court recognized the possibility of prejudice to a suspect in a pre-trial identification was real and interjected the right to counsel to guard against that possible prejudice.[28]

In *Kirby*, the defendant had been subjected to a showup without counsel following his arrest but before he was formally charged.[29] The *Kirby* Court noted that in each of the two 1967 cases the respective defendants had already been indicted when the pre-trial lineups had occurred, whereas in the case before it defendant-Kirby had not yet been formally charged.[30] The Court pointed out that the right to counsel normally becomes operative only after the "prosecution" is underway.[31] It then held that since the defendant Kirby was not yet faced with "prosecution," the right to counsel did not attach to his pre-trial identification.[32] And even though the 1967 rulings based their holdings on concerns involving eyewitness error, possible suggestiveness in the proceeding and the difficulties of later proving any prejudice the accused might have suffered, while according the fact that the defendants in these earlier cases had been formally charged basically *no* weight whatsoever,[33] the *Kirby* Court ignored the policy considerations supporting the 1967 opinions and rested their affirmance of Kirby's conviction entirely on the fact that he had been neither indicted or formally charged nor subject to the "initiation of adversary judicial criminal proceedings."[34]

If, then, the right to counsel in identification situations was originally grounded in concerns regarding avoidance of prejudice to a suspect in a lineup or showup, what difference should it make whether the identification occurred before formal charge or after formal charge? Most disconcerting about this arbitrary line of demarcation is the point that if the police know that they can ignore an arrestee's request for a lawyer before he is formally charged or taken before a judge, but cannot ignore such a request afterward, they will in most cases simply conduct their identification proceedings beforehand. In effect, the 1967 cases requiring counsel are now almost entirely meaningless. By cleverly hanging its hat on this irrelevant distinction, the *Kirby* Court essentially did away with the 1967 lineup projections without explicitly having to overrule them. Here, again, the Court delivered all the correct signals: do not cavalierly ignore *stare decisis*; allow police the discretion to conduct most of their lineups and showups without interference from defense counsel; and leave the counsel protections for formally charged defendants intact, lest they be accused of placing no control whatsoever on police misconduct. *Kirby* represents a classic illustration of how the Court took a position and ended up with the best of all worlds.

In *Kirby*, the Court laid the groundwork for focusing on the artificial distinction of whether the "prosecution" was underway in determining whether the right to counsel attached rather than on whether the defendant might suffer possible prejudice in the law enforcement effort. In one 1973 opinion, the Court used the *Kirby* test to reject right to counsel claims. In *Gagnon v. Scarpelli*,[35] the Court ruled parole and probation revocation proceedings are not "criminal prosecutions" within the meaning of the Sixth Amendment.[36]

Later, in 1973, in *United States v. Ash*,[37] the Court held the defendant's Sixth Amendment rights were not violated when a defendant's attorney was barred from observing witnesses examine a post-indictment photo array arranged by a prosecutor prior to trial.[38] Here, the Court avoided the "prosecution" text. Instead, it reasoned the "trial-like confrontation" inherent in a *Wade* lineup was not present in a pre-trial photo identification, suggested the ethical responsibilities of the prosecutor would provide a safeguard against suggestive photo arrays, and concluded the potential of prejudice to a suspect is considerably less than with the corporeal pre-trial identification.[39]

These 1973 opinions provide excellent illustrations of the Court's willingness to split hairs. With *Gagnon*, the Court's characterization of revocation proceedings as non-prosecutorial in nature is simply incorrect. At a revocation proceeding, the state must offer evidence supportive of a violation of a condition of probation or parole that, if proved, may result in resentencing of a defendant or imposition of harsher sanctions. In actuality, the operational effect of a revocation hearing may be no different than a trial and sentence. As to *Ash*, the impact of a pre-trial identification from a lineup *or* mugbook, for purposes of trial, is the same, not different. Both efforts involve the building of the government's case against a suspect. The potential problems of misidentification, suggestiveness, and after-the-fact reconstruction of the identification exercise is the same, not different. Furthermore, *Ash* ignores the fact that most pre-trial photo identifications are carried out by police, not the "ethical" prosecutor. Ignoring potential prejudice to a defendant in this context is little different than ignoring it in the *Kirby* showup.

In 1974, the Court decided *Ross v. Moffitt*,[40] where the Court dismissed an equal protection claim that a convicted indigent defendant was entitled to appointed counsel to assist him with his discretionary appeals[41] to a state supreme court and petitions for certiorari to the United States Supreme Court.[42] Although the *Ross* majority did not explicitly utilize the "prosecution" litmus test, it did use reasoning based on a similar theory. Here, the Court stated the defendant was attempting to use the attorney "not as a shield" to protect him form baseless government charges, "but rather as a sword to upset the prior determination of guilt."[43] The Court found these differential uses of counsel "significant" in denying the claim for appointed counsel in the permissive review context.[44] Of course, it might be added that this same distinction could have been used as a basis for denial of appointed counsel during the first appeal that a defendant has as a matter of right, a stage where counsel's protection does exist by virtue of a 1963 Warren Court ruling,[45] but the Court did not disturb that earlier ruling in *Moffitt*. Once again, the Court used an analysis—this time the sword/shield distinction—to suit its convenience in the permissive review situation although it had not used it in the mandatory review context.

In another 1974 case, *Wolff v. McDonnell*,[46] the Court held the injection of the right to counsel, appointed or retained, into prison disciplinary proceedings would undermine correctional goals.[47] Another case decided the same term, *Fuller v. Oregon*,[48] held a state statute that authorized a state to recoup expenditures from a *previously* indigent defendant, who the state earlier provided appointed counsel, did not constitute a chilling effect on the exercise of the right to appointed counsel.[49]

In 1975, two more right to counsel issues were resolved by the Court. In *Gerstein v. Pugh*,[50] the Court ruled the Fourth Amendment required a pre-trial right to a judicial hearing of probable cause supportive of a defendant's extended pre-trial detention.[51] However, the Court stated since this judicial inquiry did not have to be adversarial in nature, it was not a "critical stage" requiring counsel.[52] Here, the Court took the position that the possibility of continued incarceration following the judge's probable cause finding did not implicate the type of prejudice to the accused necessary to a "critical stage" finding.[53] If the absence of counsel undermines the accused's right to a *fair trial*, the Court indicated that might be a basis for finding prejudice for "critical stage" purposes.[54] Yet, if the defendant remains in jail because of an erroneous probable cause ruling made by a trial judge that might have been corrected had an attorney been present, apparently that is not prejudice for "critical stage" purposes.

Later that term, in *Faretta v. California*,[55] the Court ruled the Sixth Amendment right to counsel impliedly carries with it a right to proceed *without* counsel.[56] This case, in a sense, was a deviation from prior decisions. In earlier rulings, the Court ruled that the right to a jury trial does not confer upon a defendant the right to a trial without a jury.[57] Similarly, it had previously ruled merely because a defendant has a right to trial and a right to confront his accusers, this does not mean he has a corollary right to forego trial and instead plead guilty.[58] And, just because a defendant has a right to a public trial, he does not have a right to a private trial.[59] Notwithstanding this pattern of analysis in earlier cases, the Court here was willing to expand the scope of the Sixth Amendment protections. Of course, if one believes in the old "a fool for a client" adage, perhaps the court was not doing a service to those defendants who prefer to proceed *pro se*, but a disservice. Moreover, in no way did *Faretta* expand the right *to* counsel, appointed or retained.

A year later, the court decided *United States v. Mandujano*,[60] which addressed amongst other concerns whether a "putative" defendant called before a grand jury was entitled to counsel. Consistent with an earlier decision,[61] the Court held no right to counsel existed because no criminal proceedings had been instituted against the accused when he was subpoenaed before the grand jury to testify.[62] Here, the Court avoided the "prejudice" test, which clearly would have been more problematic in justifying its ruling, in favor of the standard that asks whether a prosecution had commenced.

In a second 1976 case, *Middendorf v. Henry*,[63] the Court held Marine enlisted men who had been charged with violations of military regulations resulting in their standing trial at summary court-martial were not being subjected to a "criminal prosecution" within the meaning of the Sixth Amendment.[64] Here, the Court held the distinctive qualities and necessities of the military outweighed other concerns including the fact that the summary court-martial could lead to loss of liberty.[65]

In a third 1976 decision, *Geders v. United States*,[66] the Court held a trial court's order preventing a defendant from consulting with his lawyer about anything during a 17-hour overnight recess in the trial between the direct examination and cross-examination of the defendant deprived the defendant of his right to the assistance of counsel.[67] While the *Geders* ruling may have appeared to be a victory for proponents of the right to counsel, its significance was minimized in the later opinion of *Perry v. Leeke*,[68] where the Court upheld such a trial court order where the cross-examination immediately followed the direct examination during the same session or where the recess between the two was brief.[69]

In 1977, in *Bounds v. Smith*,[70] the Court held the Fourteenth Amendment right to access to the courts required prison authorities to assist inmates in preparation and filing of legal papers by providing prisoners with adequate libraries to prepare their petitions on their own *or* adequate legal assistance from persons trained in the law.[71] *Bounds*, in a sense, provided good news and bad news to prison inmates. The good news was the Court was insuring that prisoners' right to access to the courts not be thwarted by lack of access to *some* type of assistance; the bad news was that assistance did not have to be a lawyer, assuming the prison provided some semblance of a law library to prisoners.

A year later, the Court reaffirmed the principle, established in a 1942 opinion,[72] that the right to counsel included the right to an attorney free of a conflict of interest. In *Holloway v. Arkansas*,[73] they held a conflict of interest had been created where an attorney retained by one defendant had been appointed to represent a co-defendant in circumstances where the two defendants had antagonistic defenses.[74] Here, timely objection was made by counsel that he could not simultaneously represent both individuals, and, accordingly, the

Supreme Court held the failure of the trial court to appoint separate counsel was violative of the Sixth Amendment even though there was no showing of actual prejudice.[75]

The final case of the decade involving a right to counsel claim was *Scott v. Illinois.*[76] In that case, an indigent defendant was charged with theft, which carried a maximum sentence of one year in jail and $500 fine, was denied the appointment of counsel, was convicted in a bench trial and received a $50 fine.[77] The Court said where the defendant was not imprisoned as a consequence of his conviction, the right to appointed counsel had not been breached.[78] Apparently, then, if a defendant suffered a conviction resulting in *any* type of fine, probation, or a suspended sentence, he has suffered no real "prejudice." For one who has lost a job or is precluded from gaining future employment, joining a profession, enlisting in the military, holding public office, or voting because of a conviction, he may be hard pressed to feel he has not been prejudiced. But so it goes.

In 1980, the United States Supreme Court affirmed the previously recognized principle that a person may not be imprisoned as a consequence of an uncounseled conviction.[79] In *Baldasar v. Illinois,*[80] the Court held a prior uncounseled misdemeanor conviction, which resulted in a fine and probation, could not be used under an enhanced penalty statute to convert a subsequent misdemeanor charge into a felony conviction carrying a prison term.[81] Here, the Court took the position that an uncounseled conviction may not only preclude imprisonment on the first conviction, but also could not be the basis for elevating a subsequent conviction to a more serious offense that would result in jail time.

That same year, the Court returned to the arena of right to counsel free of a conflict of interest in *Cuyler v. Sullivan.*[82] In that case, two privately retained attorneys represented the defendant and two co-defendants who faced murder charges.[83] In separate trials defendant Sullivan was convicted although the co-defendants were acquitted.[84] Later, the defendant argued the trial court erroneously failed to inquire into the possibility that the respective defendants had antagonistic defenses.[85] The defendant alleged he was discouraged by one of the attorneys from presenting certain evidence the defense did not want to reveal prior to the subsequent trial of the co-defendants.[86] In review, the Supreme Court noted at the outset that, unlike in *Holloway*, no claim of attorney conflict of interest was raised by any of the parties prior to trial.[87] The Court stated absent special circumstances, a trial court may safely presume multiple representation of defendants entails no conflict of interest *or* that the defendants have knowingly accepted the risks of such possible conflict.[88] In addition, the fact that in this case there were separate trials minimized the potential problems of alleged antagonistic defenses.[89] The Court concluded, in such circumstances, the burden is on the defendant to show an *actual* conflict of interest and remanded the matter to the lower court to determine if the defendant had evidence sufficient to demonstrate actual prejudice.[90] *Cuyler*, it would seem, relieved the trial court from determining whether the defendant's right to counsel has been "scrupulously honored" and shifts the burden to the defendant, at least in the possible conflict context.

The following year, the Court delivered the opinion of *Estelle v. Smith*,[91] where it ruled the Sixth Amendment required *notification* of defense counsel of a state-requested psychiatric evaluation, which would encompass the issue of the defendant's future dangerousness, that was conducted after adversary proceedings had commenced.[92] Yet, it refused to hold the defendant had a right to the assistance of appointed counsel *during* the psychiatric examination.[93] Here, they accepted the proposition that counsel's presence would add little to the examination and, instead, could seriously disrupt the examination.[94] However, the Court's refusal to extend counsel's protection into the examination itself appears to be clearly at odds with both the "prosecution" test and the "prejudice" test of the "critical stage" analysis.

In 1983, the Court issued three more right to counsel decisions. In *Morris v. Sappy*,[95] the defendant was represented by one public defender throughout most of the pre-trial proceedings.[96] However, a week before the trial the attorney was hospitalized and another public defender was assigned to the case.[97] At the opening of the trial, the defendant asserted the second public defender had insufficient time to prepare for the case and asked for a continuance, which was denied by the trial judge after the second public defender insisted he was ready for trial.[98] Following the defendant's conviction, a federal appellate court reversed on grounds the defendant had been denied a "meaningful attorney-client relationship."[99] However, the Supreme Court reversed, insisting there had been no violation of the defendant's right to counsel because a continuance was not granted, a decision that it stated was within the sound discretion of the trial court.[100] Further, the Court explicitly stated the defendant's claim that he had a right to a "meaningful relationship" with his counsel was not supported by any legal authority.[101]

In a somewhat similar case, *Jones v. Barnes*,[102] the Court held an indigent defendant had no right to demand that his appointed appellate attorney argue particular issues on appeal that the latter thought frivolous.[103] Notwithstanding the defendant's apparent feelings to the contrary, the Supreme Court determined the appellate attorney was a rigorous and effective counsel about which defendant could not complain.[104]

In a third 1983 opinion, the petitioner had no better fortune before the Court than had the previous two. In *Rushen v. Spain*,[105] the Court held the absence of counsel at a critical stage could be harmless error in certain circumstances.[106] In this case, the Court held that an ex parte communication during trial between a trial judge and a juror without notice to defendant's counsel was harmless error beyond a reasonable doubt.[107]

In 1984, in *United States v. Gouveia*,[108] the Court ruled prison inmates suspected of criminality within a prison are not entitled to the assistance of appointed counsel when they are placed in solitary confinement while prison authorities investigate their alleged criminal activity.[109] Here, the Court relied on their now familiar no "prosecution" theme.[110]

In another case decided that year, *McKaskle v. Wiggins*,[111] the Court cut back on the right to proceed *without* counsel by permitting the trial court to assign "standby counsel" to assume a role in the trial proceedings over the defendant's objection.[112] The Court ruled the involvement of standby counsel does not interfere with a defendant's right to proceed *pro se* so long as (1) the defendant retains ultimate control over his defense and (2) the jury knows the defendant chose to represent himself.[113]

However, *Gouveia* and *McKaskle* paled by comparison in terms of importance when compared against two other 1984 decisions. In *United States v. Cronic*,[114] the Court first reaffirmed its adherence to the stance that the Sixth Amendment requires the right to *effective* counsel, which means counsel must force the prosecution's case to "meaningful adversarial testing."[115] However, the Court stated the lawyer is *presumed* competent and the burden is on the accused to demonstrate otherwise.[116] In a companion case, *Strickland v. Washington*,[117] the Court explained the elements necessary to show incompetence: (1) defendant must prove that counsel was not a reasonably effective advocate, *and* (2) counsel's performance, in the case at hand, actually prejudiced the outcome of the proceeding.[118] The Court stated merely because counsel chose a particular strategic course of action that in hindsight might not have been the preferred avenue of defense does not undermine a finding of competence unless the defendant would in all likelihood have been exonerated but for counsel's error or errors.[119]

Although the *Cronic* and *Strickland* decisions might have first appeared to offer useful protections against incompetent counsel, the two-prong *Strickland* test will generally prove to be very difficult to satisfy in a given case. To illustrate, suppose a defense counsel determines it would be strategically disadvantageous to have the defendant testify in his own defense because, for example, the defendant's prior criminal conviction may be brought out during the state's cross-examination of the defendant. If the defendant is thereafter convicted primarily because the jury never heard the defendant's own exculpatory claims, the defendant will likely fail with his incompetence claim since the decision not to put the defendant in the witness box may have been a "reasonable" option at the time. In other words, since the counsel's decisions may have been objectively reasonable and counsel himself is presumed competent in his decision-making, his representation will be considered competent even though in fact his erroneous decision may have affected the outcome of the case. Here, defendant fails because of his failure to satisfy the first prong of *Strickland.*

Even more interesting is the second part of the *Strickland* standard. To illustrate, suppose defendant was represented by counsel who made numerous errors during the defendant's trial or entirely failed to challenge the prosecution's case with "meaningful adversarial testing." However, the state placed into evidence the defendant's valid confession, which most likely was the primary basis upon which the jury rested its verdict of guilty. Now, the defendant will fail because he failed to satisfy the second prong of the *Strickland* standard. In other words, even though counsel may have been entirely inept as measured by the first part of *Strickland,* the defendant's conviction will be affirmed by the appellate court because the defendant would have in all likelihood been convicted anyway because of the confession.

A year later, the Court decided two other cases involving claims of incompetency of counsel. In *Hill v. Lockhart,*[120] the Court ruled the *Strickland* test applied to counsel's advise that his client should forego trial and plead guilty.[121] In this case, the Court affirmed the defendant's convictions, despite the erroneous advise he received from his counsel regarding his eligibility for parole, since he failed to demonstrate how he was prejudiced when he was sentenced to a statutorily required prison term that precluded eligibility for parole until later than he anticipated.[122]

Meanwhile, in *Evitts v. Lucey,*[123] the Court ruled the due process clause of the Fourteenth Amendment required the right to effective counsel in a defendant's first appeal, which he enjoys as a matter of right.[124] Here, the Court affirmed a lower court reversal of the defendant's conviction because his attorney failed to file a timely "statement of appeal" as required by state law.[125]

In 1986, the Court returned to its pattern of rejecting most Sixth Amendment claims in the case of *Murray v. Carrier.*[126] In that case, the Court held a defendant's failure to raise in state court of review a possible incompetency claim barred a federal court from considering such a claim under a petition for federal habeas corpus.[127] In *Nix v. Whitehead*,[128] the Court ruled an attorney had not provided constitutionally deficient representation by refusing to allow a defendant from committing perjury.[129] In *Darden v. Wainwright*,[130] the Court held counsel's performance was not constitutionally inept when he failed to introduce evidence in mitigation at the defendant's capital sentencing hearing and instead relied on the defendant's personal plea for mercy, a decision the Court wrote off as merely "strategic."[131] On the other hand, in *Kimmelman v. Morrison*,[132] the Court found the incompetence prong of *Strickland* violated a defendant's rights where a defendant's attorney exhibited a "startling ignorance of the law."[133] In that case, counsel had failed to file a motion to suppress evidence prior to trial as required by law, had totally failed to conduct pre-trial discovery, and admitted he did not realize the prosecution had the authority to proceed on a charge that the victim did not want to prosecute.[134] Here, the Court could not pigeonhole counsel's failures as "strategy," for it was evident from the record that counsel was simply unaware of these fundamental aspects of criminal procedure.[135]

Darden and *Kimmelman* in particular are quite instructive as to a petitioner's hurdles in proving incompetency. If counsel fails to argue certain points or fails to follow certain procedures, his unorthodox behavior will usually not be deemed constitutionally inept if there is nothing in the record to suggest he was unaware of the alternative courses of action. Common sense would dictate most attorneys will not admit to such malfeasance, and, accordingly, an appellate court may dismiss the less than preferable representation as a mere choice of strategy.

In 1987, in *Pennsylvania v. Finley*,[136] the Court ruled claims for a right to *appointed* counsel do not extend to mounting a *collateral* attack on a defendant's conviction.[137] This decision was not surprising in light of the Court's earlier decision of *Ross v. Moffit*,[138] where the Burger Court refused to extend cost-free counsel to petitioners whose requests for review were beyond the first appeal, which defendants enjoy as a matter of right.

In another case decided that year, *Burger v. Kemp*,[139] the Court entertained and rejected a defendant's claim the he was represented by counsel who had (1) a conflict of interest and (2) not been competent.[140] Here, the Court ruled even though a co-defendant had been represented by the partner of defendant's counsel and defendant's counsel assisted his partner in that representation, there was no showing of actual prejudice.[141] Further, the Court ruled the failure of defendant's counsel to develop and present any mitigating circumstances at the defendant's capital sentencing hearing was supported by the reasonable professional judgement standard of *Strickland*.[142]

In 1988, the Court ruled in *Wheat v. United States*[143] a defendant had no Sixth Amendment right to be represented by the same attorney as his two co-defendants in a drug conspiracy where the trial court had determined such representation might constitute a conflict of interest.[144] Here, the Court held while there exists a presumption in favor of a defendant's retained counsel of choice, this presumption could be overcome by a "demonstatration of actual conflict" or a "serious potential for conflict."[145]

That same term, the Court decided *Satterwhite v. Texas*,[146] wherein the Court entertained a Sixth Amendment claim that a defendant's rights had been violated when a psychiatrist conducted an examination of the defendant to determine his future dangerousness without *notifying* defendant's counsel[147] as required by *Estelle v. Smith*.[48] Specifically, the Court considered whether an *Estelle* violation could ever be harmless error and whether it was harmless error in this case.[149] First, the Court ruled *Estelle* violations could be harmless error in an appropriate case[150] but, second, held it was not harmless error in this case since the findings at the psychiatric examination were critical to the defendant's ultimate sentence to death.[151] Here, again, the Court's ruling was not much of a victory for Sixth Amendment claimants. *Satterwhite* simply reaffirmed the *Estelle* proposition that defendant's counsel be *notified* about the examination in order to consult with his client. It did not state a defendant had the right to the *presence* of counsel while the psychiatrist was making his critical assessment. More importantly, the Court narrowed the *Estelle* protection, for whatever it is worth, by adding the dimension of a harmless error analysis to such claims, an issue never addressed in *Estelle* itself.

In 1989, the Court literally dropped a bomb on the right to *retained* counsel. In *Caplin and Drysdale v. United States*,[152] a defense attorney representing a defendant charged with narcotics violations challenged a federal drug proceeds forfeiture statute used to restrain the defendant from transferring funds prior to trial to his lawyer for his legal services.[153] The Court held that statute was constitutional and its provisions did not infringe on a defendant's right to counsel of his choice.[154] Similarly, in *United States v. Monsanto*,[155] the Court held a defendant charged with federal RICO violations could not transfer funds that were frozen by reason of a federal forfeiture statute nor claim such inability to use these funds to hire an attorney of his choice violated his right to counsel.[156] These cases clearly create a pandora's box for attorneys who are prepared to represent defendants charged with crime where government pre-trial forfeiture provisions may bar transferring of funds from a client to his attorney. With the dramatic growth of forfeiture statutes directed against criminals, the right to retained counsel could become totally meaningless in the future. For example, suppose a state passed a law that states all persons charged with theft-related charges—robbery, extortion, burglary, larceny, and the like—are now to face pre-trial asset-freezing forfeiture provisions under the guise that such is necessary to return to the rightful owner the value of the losses suffered by the theft victim. Or suppose a jurisdiction passed a law that all persons charged with crimes against persons—murder, manslaughter, battery, assault, kidnapping, and so forth—shall be subject to similar pre-trial forfeiture actions on the pretense that such is necessary to insure that the victim or the victim's family will be properly compensated for their injuries or loss. It does not take a genius to determine the implications on the right to counsel of choice could be devastating to persons *charged* with crimes. What incentive will remain for the private bar to handle criminal cases except for those with a *pro bono* bent? And, if such occurs, what happens to the defendant's presumption of innocence? And what happens to the defendant's other constitutional protections, such as his Sixth Amendment right to confront his accusers? Surely, the defenders of the forfeiture of attorney's fees cases will retort that the defendant will at least be entitled to appointed counsel if his funds have been gobbled up by a government forfeiture action. However, one then must ask how will the already overburdened and underfinanced public defender systems throughout the country possibly handle this new group of cases that were previously handled by the private bar?

Finally, the Court quite literally placed a nail in the coffin of death row petitioners desirous of counsel in their decision of *Murray v. Giarratano.*[157] In that case, the Court held neither the Eighth Amendment prohibition against cruel and unusual punishment nor the due process clause required states to provide appointed counsel for indigent death row inmates who were seeking postconviction collateral relief.[158] Considering that the lives of indigent petitioners are literally on the line, one might have thought the Court would deviate from its stance taken in *Ross v. Moffit,*[159] but the Court stood firm on its niggardly approach to requests for appointed counsel in collateral review situations.

As with the other procedural protections discussed earlier, a clear pattern of denials of a meaningful right to counsel emerged during the Burger and Rehnquist Court periods. Where the Court seemingly expands, at least at first glance, on the right to counsel, one finds upon closer scrutiny that these alleged extensions of the right are largely illusory. The right to "effective" counsel decisions, such as *Strickland*, are an excellent example if one studies the difficult standard that a defendant must satisfy before he or she is provided relief. The right to proceed *without* counsel, supported by *Faretta*, is a hollow right if one considers the dangers and disadvantages associated with *pro se* representation.

Other "expansions" of the right during this post-Warren Court era offer only minimal protections. The *Geders* pronouncement regarding a defendant's right to confer with counsel during an overnight recess between his own direct and cross-examination will provide little comfort to the average defendant. The *Estelle* right to have counsel notified about the scheduled psychiatric interview *prior* to a court-ordered psychiatric examination will likely provide little solace to an emotionally or psychologically troubled defendant who alone will have to face the psychiatrist's penetrating questioning during the actual psychiatric interview. And, a decision like *Bounds* that conditions a prison inmate's right to counsel on the absence of some type of law library in the institution is not very significant given the existence of skeleton law libraries in many, if not most, penal institutions.

Meanwhile, where those requests for counsel, appointed or retained, affect large numbers of defendants, the Court normally retreats from the constitutional demand that a defendant has a right to counsel in "all criminal prosecutions." The *Kirby* ruling regarding the existence of no right to counsel during a lineup conducted prior to a formal charge, the *Ross* holding regarding the absence of a right to appointed counsel in discretionary appeals, the *Finley* ruling regarding no right to appointed counsel in collateral review situations, the *Giarratano* denial of appointed counsel for death row inmates who are seeking collateral relief, the *Gerstein* statement that no right to counsel need be accorded a defendant while a trial judge makes the critical determination as to whether there exists probable cause to detain the defendant prior to trial, the *Gagnon* decision that denies a probation or parole revocation hearing is a critical stage, and the *Caplin* and *Monsanto* rulings that *alleged* illicit drug profiteers have no right to counsel of their choice are all examples of quite important procedural settings where the court has turned its head away from a defendant's claim that he should have had the support of someone trained in the law.

The *Gideon* ruling and its progeny decided during the tenure of Chief Justice Earl Warren were premised on the reality that a defendant would be at a decided disadvantage if he were forced to proceed alone against the government with its almost infinite resources that can be used to build a case against a suspect, prosecute and convict him, and ward off any appellate and collateral challenges he might make against such a conviction. These opinions implicitly recognized that individual liberties are sacred, and, thus, they commenced to build a foundation of procedural protections designed to assure that an accused is truly accorded due process of law when he is faced with the criminal justice system.

While the Warren Court was criticized for providing defendants unnecessary "technicalities," in reality the Burger Court and, later, the Rehnquist Court developed some technicalities of their own in order to bring to a halt the building of the full panalopy of protections that the Warren Court obviously had in mind. For example, by focusing on when a "prosecution" was underway and by interpretating that term as arising only after a defendant was faced with a "formal" charge, the latter courts were placing form over substance. Further, by resorting to rhetoric of the highest order, as in *Ross* where Justice Rehnquist stated counsel could be used as a "shield" but not a "sword," many portions of these later opinions at some times sound more like the speeches of law-and-order politicians than the language one might expect from the so-called guardians of our Bill of Rights.

But, more to the point, in the Burger and Rehnquist opinions involving right to counsel claims, the Court can be seen for what it has become—the creators of an illusion. In all too many of these decisions, the opinion begins with a recital of the litany of *earlier* Warren Court rulings where the respective petitioners' claims *were* recognized, complete with references to "fundamental" rights, basic "protections," and other similar platitudes. In a sense, these case law introductions to the subject at hand appear to be an exercise by the court to pat itself on the back as the nation's ultimate champion of civil liberties. But as the opinion begins to analyze the problem at hand, the rationale supporting the court's retreat from the petitioner's claim begins to talk shape. Distinctions are offered. An exception is developed. The petitioner's claim that he needs the guiding hand of counsel is rejected. His conviction is affirmed. The Court sings its praises to the Constitution. Behind the singing, the Court adds a repertoire of symbols to *Gideon's* lone trumpet.

> Defendant has rights;
> plenty of rights.
> But this complaint is wrong,
> and we the Court are right.
> Civil liberties affirmed.
> Defendant's conviction affirmed.
> Nothing is wrong;
> everything is right.

Gideon's trumpet is drowned out by the sounds of the symphony. Symbols over substance. Rhetoric over reason. And the band plays on.

NOTES

1. 372 U.S. 335 (1963).
2. Betts v. Brady, 316 U.S. 455 (1942) ("[W]e cannot say that the [Fourteenth] amendment embodies an inexorable command that no trial for any offense, or in any court, can be fairly conducted and justice accorded a defendant who is not represented by counsel").
3. *Id.* at 343–45.
4. 372 U.S. at 344.
5. *Id.* at 345, quoting Powell v. Alabama, 387 U.S. 45, 69 (1932).
6. Anthony Lewis, GIDEON'S TRUMPET (1964).
7. Arthur J. Goldberg, EQUAL JUSTICE: THE WARREN ERA OF THE SUPREME COURT, 10–11 (1971).
8. Those proceeding where the right exists have normally been described a "critical stage." A "critical stage" exists if (1) some prejudice to the defendant's rights inheres in the particular procedural context and (2) counsel might help avoid that prejudice. United States v. Wade, 388 U.S. 218 (1967).
9. Miranda v. Arizona, 384 U.S. 436 (1966) (custodial interrogation); Escobedo v. Arizona, 378 U.S. 478 (1963) (where interrogation becomes accusatory).
10. United States v. Wade, 388 U.S. 218 (1967); Gilbert v. California, 388 U.S. 263 (1967).
11. Coleman v. Alabama, 399 U.S. 1 (1970).
12. White v. Maryland, 373 U.S. 59 (1963).
13. Gideon v. Wainwright, 372 U.S. 335 (1963).
14. *In re* Gault, 387 U.S. 1 (1967).
15. Mempa v. Rhay, 389 U.S. 128 (1967).
16. Douglas v. California, 372 U.S. 353 (1963) (decided on equal protection grounds).
17. Argersinger v. Hamlin, 407 U.S. 25 (1972).
18. Boyd v. Dutton, 405 U.S. 1, 2–3 (1972) (during guilty plea proceeding).
19. 406 U.S. 682 (1972) (plurality).
20. United States v. Wade, 388 U.S. 218 (1967); Gilbert v. California, 388 U.S. 263 (1967).
21. 388 U.S. 218 (1967).
22. *Id.* at 228.
23. *Id.*
24. *Id.* at 229.
25. *Id.* at 230–32.

26. *Id.* at 227.

27. *Id.* at 226.

28. *Id.* at 236–38.

29. 406 U.S. at 684–90.

30. *Id.* at 687–90.

31. However, the Court conceded the right to counsel did become operative in certain police interrogation situations, which normally occur before the investigation is turned over to the prosecution. *Id.* at 689.

32. *Id.* at 690.

33. *See* United States v. Wade, 388 U.S. 218 (1967); Gilbert v. California, 388 U.S. 263 (1967).

34. 406 U.S. at 689.

35. 411 U.S. 778 (1973).

36. *Id.* at 782.

37. 413 U.S. 300 (1973).

38. *Id.* at 303.

39. *Id.* at 312–21.

40. 417 U.S. 600 (1974).

41. Discretionary or permissible review may occur beyond the first appeal to the intermediate appellate court, which first appeal a defendant enjoys as a matter of right. The first appeal is protected by the right to counsel by reason of equal protection. Douglas v. California, 372 U.S. 353 (1963). Discretionary review involves that stage of review where the reviewing court may or may not give full consideration to the alleged claims of error. *See* Robert L. Stern, APPELLATE PRACTICE IN THE UNITED STATES, secs. 5.1—5.10 (1981).

42. 417 U.S. at 610, 616–18.

43. *Id.* at 610–11.

44. *Id.* at 610.

45. Douglas v. California, 372 U.S. 353 (1963).

46. 418 U.S. 539 (1974).

47. *Id.* at 570.

48. 417 U.S. 40 (1974).

49. *Id.* at 51–54. The claim dismissed in *Fuller* was based on an equal protection argument.

50. 420 U.S. 103 (1975).

51. *Id.* at 114.

52. *Id.* at 122.

53. *Id.* at 123.

54. *See id.* at 122–23.

55. 422 U.S. 806 (1975).

56. *Id.* at 818–32.

57. Singer v. United States, 380 U.S. 24 (1965).

58. North Carolina v. Alford, 400 U.S. 25 (1975).

59. Singer v. United States, 380 U.S. 24, 35 (1965) (dictum).

60. 425 U.S. 564 (1976) (plurality).

61. *In re* Groban, 352 U.S. 330, 333 (1957).

62. 425 U.S. at 581.

63. 425 U.S. 25 (1976).
64. *Id.* at 34.
65. *Id.* at 33–42.
66. 425 U.S. 80 (1976).
67. *Id.* at 91.
68. 109 S. Ct. 594 (1989).
69. *Id.* at 602.
70. 430 U.S. 817 (1977).
71. *Id.* at 828.
72. Glasser v. United States, 315 U.S. 60 (1942).
73. 435 U.S. 475 (1978).
74. *Id.* at 476–78.
75. *Id.* at 483–91. Here, counsel refused to reveal to the trial court the basis of the conflict on grounds the information was privileged.
76. 440 U.S. 367 (1979).
77. *Id.* at 368.
78. *Id.* at 373–74.
79. See Argersinger v. Hamlin, 407 U.S. 25 (1972).
80. 446 U.S. 222 (1980) (per curiam).
81. *Id.* at 224 (Stewart, J., concurring); *id.* at 225–26 (Marshall, J., concurring); *id.* at 230 (Blackmun, J., concurring).
82. 446 U.S. 335 (1980).
83. *Id.* at 337.
84. *Id.* at 338.
85. *Id.* at 345.
86. *Id.* at 338–339.
87. *Id.* at 347.
88. *Id.* at 346–47.
89. *Id.* at 347.
90. *Id.* at 348–50.
91. 451 U.S. 454 (1981).
92. *Id.* at 470–71.
93. *Id.* at 470, n. 14.
94. *Id.*
95. 461 U.S. 1 (1983).
96. *Id.* at 5.
97. *Id.*
98. *Id.* at 6.
99. *Id.* at 10–11.
100. *Id.* at 11–12.
101. *Id.* at 12–14.
102. 463 U.S. 745 (1983).
103. *Id.* at 750–54.
104. *Id.* at 754.
105. 464 U.S. 114 (1983) (per curiam).
106. *Id.* at 117–20.
107. *Id.* at 120–21.
108. 467 U.S. 180 (1984).

109. *Id.* at 192.
110. *See id.* at 187–92.
111. 465 U.S. 168 (1984).
112. *Id.* at 176–88.
113. *Id.* at 178.
114. 466 U.S. 648 (1984).
115. *Id.* at 656.
116. *Id.* at 658.
117. 466 U.S. 668 (1984).
118. *Id.* at 687.
119. *Id.* at 689.
120. 474 U.S. 52 (1985).
121. *Id.* at 58.
122. *Id.* at 60. The Court reasoned the defendant never alleged he would have failed to plead guilty and insisted on a trial had he known that he would not have been eligible for parole until later. *Id.*
123. 469 U.S. 387 (1985).
124. *Id.* at 396.
125. *Id.* at 389–91.
126. 477 U.S. 478 (1986).
127. *Id.* at 488–89 (federal habeas corpus exhaustion doctrine requires claims of ineffective assistance of counsel be presented to state courts as independent claim before alleged incompetence may be used to establish cause for procedural default).
128. 475 U.S. 157 (1986).
129. *Id.* at 173–74.
130. 477 U.S. 168 (1986).
131. *Id.* at 184–87.
132. 477 U.S. 365 (1986).
133. *Id.* at 385.
134. *Id.*
135. *Id.*
136. 481 U.S. 551 (1987).
137. *Id.* at 555.
138. 417 U.S. 600 (1974).
139. 483 U.S. 776 (1987).
140. *Id.* at 777–78.
141. *Id.* at 783–88.
142. *Id.* at 788–95.
143. 108 S. Ct. 1692 (1988).
144. *Id.* at 1697.
145. *Id.* at 1700.
146. 108 S. Ct. 1792 (1988).
147. *Id.* at 1794–95.
148. 451 U.S. 454 (1981).
149. 108 S. Ct. at 1795.
150. *Id.* at 1797–98.
151. *Id.* at 1798–99.

152. 109 S. Ct. 2646 (1989).
153. *Id.* at 2649–51.
154. *Id.* at 2651–56.
155. 109 S. Ct. 2657 (1989).
156. *Id.* at 2665–67.
157. 109 S. Ct. 2765 (1989).
158. *Id.* at 2769–72.
159. 417 U.S. 600 (1974).

CHAPTER 6

Judicial Conservatism, Crime Control, and Other Current Myths

THE WARREN COURT was *correctly* accused of being defenders of the rights of criminals: not defenders of their right to commit crime as some Warren Court critics cynically implied, but defenders of their right to due process. This Court recognized the Founding Fathers had established a governmental arrangement where rights were not reserved to those only engaged in legitimate pursuits, such as practicing one's religion, for language within the Bill of Rights explicitly speaks of the rights of the "accused."[1] Even *convicted* offenders were provided rights as the bar against "cruel and unusual punishment" makes clear.[2] When confronted with the constitutional scheme that it had inherited, the Warren Court took steps, for which it was severely criticized.[3] These steps were designed to achieve two goals. First, the Court wanted to assure those rights were equally available to not just the rich, but also the poor; not merely to those with understanding, but also the uninformed; not only those facing the forces of the federal government, but also the state. Second, the Court wanted to insure the citizenry that the promises afforded them in the Bill of Rights provide not lip service protection from government excess, but instead *meaningful protection against summary process as well as baseless charge.* Their role in this constitutional arrangement was to be the guarantors of due process. This was the Court's constitutional *duty*, as defenders of the Bill of Rights. Who could argue with this? Nonetheless, the crime control establishment challenged the Warren Court's exercise of constitutional authority, often dubbing the Warren Court as radical or revolutionary. Whether one agrees or disagrees with the Court's constitutional interpretation during this period, few would challenge the point as Herbert Packer observed over twenty years ago, namely, the Warren Court elevated the due process model of criminal justice that embraced fairness, equity, and the presumption of innocence above the crime control model that espoused efficiency, finality, and the presumption of guilt.[4]

Since about 1970, a new order of constitutional interpretation has appeared in the criminal procedure arena. This observer thinks it evident that the Burger and Rehnquist Court majorities, respectively, have engaged in a pattern of decision-making designed to contain and, more often, strangle the lifeblood of the due process model. The preceding review of the twenty-plus years of opinions involving the exclusionary rule, search and seizure, *Miranda,* and the right to counsel amply support this proposition. Even Justice Stevens has suggested that the Court may have "become a loyal footsoldier in the Executive's fight on crime."[5] Of course, due process concerns have not totally evaporated into thin air. However, since the new crime control establishment has attracted a majority of the Court into its corner, the Court now treats due process concerns that significantly strain crime control like most Americans approach inclement weather: one talks about it, but never completely avoiding its impact, one does the *utmost* to try.

It is posited, here, that the Court today has a priority scheme significantly different from the Warren Court in the due process–crime control tug of war Professor Packer so eloquently described over two decades ago. And if it is fair to describe the Warren Court's clear effort in favor of the due process model as "revolutionary" or "radical" to the left, then it is equally appropriate to characterize the Burger and Rehnquist Courts' obvious movement of the pendulum toward the crime control model with similar epitaphs: radical, counterrevolutionary, or, simply revolutionary to the right.

At this juncture, one might ask what is the point of this observer's above characterization of the Burger and Rehnquist Courts' efforts in the last couple decades? Mere cynical name-calling? Quite simply, it is to make the obvious point that the latter Court's *alteration of priorities*—elevating the question of guilt over the question of process—*is as significant and important to the criminal justice system as was the Warren Court's movement in the opposite direction.* Whether the Court has now landed its feet in a new position that is "moderate," "conservative," or the like is not this author's point. Any such labeling can only be an exercise in semantics. It is important to realize *profound change* in constitutional criminal procedure *has continued* during the post-Warren Court period. Judicial activism is not a figment of the history of the Court during the 1950s and 1960s. Judicial activism is alive and kicking today. It has only changed directions. Its new course was seized by and now serves those with a more conservative political agenda. The notion that judicial conservatism exists today is a myth.

Whether one agrees or disagrees with this change in emphasis in constitutional criminal procedure law, the *fact that change has occurred is undeniable.* If one merely focuses on the four topics of criminal procedure in this study, it is apparent the Burger and Rehnquist Court eras cannot be described as periods of status quo. The expansion of the limitations and exceptions on the reach of the exclusionary rule obviously opens the door to greater constitutional *tolerance* of police and judicial error in evidence gathering.[6] While these modifications of the exclusionary rule impact generally, even if not inevitably, on the rights of those who harbor evidence of crime, the developments in Fourth Amendment jurisprudence impact on the freedom of all Americans. While the "public exposure" doctrine emasculates the citizen's expectation of "privacy," the scales of the "reasonableness" balance more often give way to imperatives of "crime control."[7] Searches are no longer "searches." The warrant clause and the "probable cause" standard become the exception rather than the rule when a search *is* recognized as a "search." In the interest of identifying the criminality of a few, all of us suffer a loss of freedom from needless government inquiry. The *Miranda* doctrine, designed to assure meaningful and intelligent waivers of the right of suspects to remain silent during custodial police interrogation, becomes a "prophylactic device" with a sufficient number of holes in it that no longer offers complete protection.[8] And the *Gideon* promise regarding the protections of legal counsel, appointed or retained, in all stages of the criminal justice system often becomes a hollow promise in critical settings.[9] While many might salute these developments in constitutional criminal procedure as necessary to the "war on crime," one might ask whether the turn in direction taken by our constitutional law is a healthy one.

This is not a time to become complacent about due process and the "rights" of those suspected or accused of crime. Witness the unprovoked savage police beatings of alleged suspects that has recently been captured on video tape.[10] The use of unjustified physical force, including torture, is all too common a police tactic in the police quest to solve crime.[11] Not surprisingly, many citizens fear for their safety in *any* encounter with the police.[12] Governmental surveillance, including use of the most sophisticated devices technology affords,[13] is directed at criminals and law-abiding citizens alike.[14] Citizens often seek protection *from* those who have the duty to protect them.

Visit many of our criminal courts and observe assembly-line criminal process. Crowded court dockets undermine the quality of justice.[15] Indigent defendants often experience poor legal representation by understaffed public defenders.[16] Although plea bargaining serves a vital function, justice is undeniably compromised[17] as it causes the great majority of defendants to forgo their exercise of their constitutional rights—to a trial, to a jury, to confront ones accusers, and to subpoena favorable witnesses—in the interest of gaining a reduction in the charges, a reduced sentence, or other benefits.[18] When one carefully examines the police and courts in action, it is difficult to lay the blame on our concerns for fundamental freedoms and due process.

In 1986, the American Bar Association Section on Criminal Justice appointed the Special Committee on Criminal Justice in a Free Society to study the impact of constitutional protections on crime control. In a 1988 report entitled *Criminal Justice in Crisis*, the committee found the major problem in crime control was a lack of resources that the criminal justice system needs to detect crime and bring that crime into the criminal justice system.[19] For example, they found in 1986 that approximately 31 million of the 34 million serious crimes committed against persons or property were either never reported or never solved.[20] Often the criminal perpetrator never even encounters the criminal justice system.

> Because constitutional protections affect so few persons involved in crime, they cannot be blamed for our crime problem. This makes all the more fraudulent the myth spread by some political leaders that the exclusionary rule and *Miranda* prevent the police from protecting the public against crime. These politicians use the Bill of Rights as a scapegoat for their own failure to address the crime problem honestly.[21]

Also, the public at large is to blame. While the populace demands curbs on the level of crime, it is not prepared to bear the cost of more resources for police, prosecution, criminal defense, courts, and corrections as well as expenditures necessary to address the roots of crime: poverty, unemployment, lack of education, and the like.[22]

Thus, the politicians and public alike who believed the adoption of a "tough-on-crime" philosophy by the nation's highest court during the Burger and Rehnquist years would significantly alter the level of criminality were proven wrong.[23]

There is a sad irony here. While the Court curbs Fourth, Fifth, and Sixth Amendment freedoms, it simultaneously limits the protections of habeas corpus,[24] approves[25] and expedites[26] the business of capital punishment, accepts preventive detention,[27] and elsewhere sacrifices our fundamental freedom in the name of crime control. Thus it is appropriate to ask what have these changes produced in terms of crime control *results*? If it is fair to ask, as did the majority of the Court recently, whether a particular feature of a due process claim would "seriously impede effective law enforcement,"[28] it seems entirely reasonable to pose a cost-benefit analysis form of question the Burger and Rehnquist Courts have used to their advantage. Simply put: where a particular prosecutorial objective carries little, if any, discernible benefit in crime control, should the objective be given constitutional approval where it might seriously impede due process? What Brandeis, Holmes, Warren, Douglas, Brennan, Marshall, and others of their perspective on due processed realized, and what the Burger and Rehnquist majorities apparently fail to understand, is that adherence to a due process model exacts a price that history has demonstrated is worth paying. Today, as numerous peoples throughout the world struggle to emulate the democratic model that we Americans enjoy, complete with proclivities toward excess, *they* understand too much freedom and too many rights are vastly preferable to too little. *They* have experienced how government without appropriate checks and balances can jail or imprison for little or no reason with complete immunity. *They* understand a "trial" of an accused may be a meaningless charade. *They* understand the mechanics of an inquisitorial model of government. *They* know about the potential for tyranny amongst the powerful majority. *They* appreciate why good government protects the weak from the strong. *They* realize that, yes, one can stand wrongly accused and, thus, it is better to provide that individual with too many days in court than too few.

It seems ironic that as those peoples struggle to have more human rights, a politically powerful conservative force that has controlled the White House most of the last twenty-five years, and now the United States Supreme Court, is clearly bent on still more limitations on human rights in various legal arenas including that of criminal procedure. Today they suggest we totally ditch the exclusionary rule, abolish *Miranda*, further limit the availability of federal habeas corpus protections, and "give the police more powers" in their "war" on crime, whatever that means. As often occurs in a war, truth is the first casualty. In this "war on crime," the wounding of specific constitutional protections have become a second casualty. Tomorrow, who can guess? Will this group that also seems to have a penchant for constitutional amendments—prayer in school, abortion, balanced budget, flag burning, et cetera—bring about in the name of crime control the demise of the privilege against self-incrimination?

There are ominous clouds on the horizon of constitutional law that strongly suggest a strategy that will make the Court's revolution toward the right complete. In 1987, in *Booth v. Maryland*,[29] and again in 1989, in *South Carolina v. Gathers*,[30] the United States Supreme Court ruled the Eighth Amendment bar against cruel and unusual punishment prohibited the admission of "victim impact" evidence in a capital sentencing hearing where the state is requesting the imposition of the death penalty. In both cases, the Court reasoned admitting evidence of a murder victim's character and the impact of

the murder on the victim's family, where the defendant was unaware
of the personal circumstances of his victim, would be to introduce
"factors . . . wholly unrelated to the blameworthiness of [the] particular
defendant."[31] And even where the defendant was familiar with these
personal circumstances of his victim, focusing on these concerns might
prejudice the jury and prevent them from pursuing their obligation
of examining the character of the *defendant* and the circumstances
of his crime.[32] There was danger of contributing to arbitrariness in
the imposition of the ultimate punishment, because of coincidences
of whether the victim had left behind a family, whether and to what
extent they expresses their grief, and whether they enjoyed status
in the community.[33]

However in 1991, in *Payne v. Tennessee*,[34] the Court reconsidered
its holdings in the 1987 and 1989 opinions, ultimately ruling the
victim impact evidence *was* admissible in the penalty phase of a capital
trial. Not nearly as important as the holding itself was the Court's
analysis that could be used in future cases to demolish much, if not
all, of what remains of the due process model built by the Warren
Court.

When Chief Justice Rehnquist, writing for the Court in *Payne*,
made his case in favor of admission of victim impact statements in
capital sentencing hearings, echoing arguments that appeared in the
Booth and *Gathers* dissenting opinions, one might simply observe
that different minds might differ on this difficult question.[35] But what
followed this discussion in his opinion was of bombshell magnitude.
When confronted with the argument that principle of *stare decisis*
should preclude the Court from tampering with its 1987 and 1989
rulings on the matter, he responded that *stare decisis* "is not an
inexorable command" but instead a "principle of policy."[36] Under the
policy, he explained, "[it is] more important that the applicable rule
of law be settled than it be settled right."[37] *Stare decisis* principles
are at their weakest point in "constitutional cases," he said, because
correction through legislative initiative is virtually impossible.[38]

> Considerations in favor of *stare decisis* are at their acme in cases
> involving property and contract rights, where reliance interests are
> involved, . . . the opposite is true in cases such as the present one
> involving procedural and evidentiary rules.[38]

Here, the two prior decisions involving victim impact statements had
been "decided by the narrowest of margins, over spirited
dissents, . . . have been questioned by members of the Court in later
decisions, and have defied consistent application by the lower courts."[40]

In *Payne*, Justice Marshall wrote one of his last and most stinging dissents insisting that, "[p]ower, not reason, is the currency of this Court's decision making."[41] In explaining the result in *Payne*, he wrote:

> In dispatching *Booth* and *Gathers* to their graves today's majority ominously suggests that an even more extensive upheaval of this Court's precedents may be in store. Renouncing this Court's historical committment to a conception of "the judiciary as a source of impersonal reasoned judgments," the majority declares itself free to discard any principle of constitutional liberty which was recognized or reaffirmed over the dissenting votes of four justices and with which five or more justices *now* disagree. The implications of this radical new exception to the doctrine of *stare decisis* are staggering. The majority sends a clear signal that scores of established constitutional liberties are ripe for reconsideration, thereby inviting the very type of open defiance that the majority rewards in this case.[42]

The Court, said Marshall, "never departed from precedent" without "special justification," such as changed circumstances that "undermine a decision's rationale."[43] Here, "[it] takes little detective work to discern just what *was* changed since this Court decided *Booth* and *Gathers*: this Court's own personnel."[44]

Justice Marshall continued his verbal assault on the majority when he addressed the Court's new policy regarding precedent.

> This truncation of the Court's duty to stand by its own precedents is astonishing. By limiting full protection of the doctrine of *stare decisis* to "cases involving property and contract rights," . . . the majority sends a clear signal that essentially *all* decisions implementing the personal liberties protected by the Bill of Rights and the Fourteenth Amendment are open to reexamination. Taking into account the majority's additional criterion for overruling—that a case either was decided or reaffirmed by a 5–4 margin "over spirited dissent"—the continued utility of literally scores of decision must be understood to depend on nothing more than proclivities of the individuals who now comprise a majority of this Court.[45]

Payne illustrates the current state of affairs in constitutional criminal procedure. No longer must the Court's majority rely on reason and rationale. To borrow words from Justice Marshall, it is now a matter of "power" and which "personnel" have it. The majority's agenda in this area of the law, like the conduct of the government in the name of the "war on crime" is, again borrowing language from Justice Marshall, often nothing short of "radical." The Court's continual sidestepping of precedent that can be argued to equal overturning such precedent may make the due process remedies meaningless. Together the Burger and Rehnquist Courts *have* accomplished what the due process proponents have feared and the crime control advocates have called for, each in the name of criminal justice—a revolution to the right.

NOTES

1. U.S. Const. Amend. VI.
2. U.S. Const. Amend. VI.
3. *See* Chapter 1, notes 35–38 *supra* and accompanying text.
4. *See* Chapter 1, notes 33–34 *supra* and accompanying text.
5. California v. Accevedo, 111 S. Ct. 1982, 2002 (1991) (Stevens, J., dissenting).
6. *See* Chapter 2, *supra*.
7. *See* Chapter 3, *supra*.
8. *See* Chapter 4, *supra*.
9. *See* Chapter 5, *supra*.
10. *See* Lance Morrow, *Rough Justice*, TIME, Apr. 1, 1991, at 16, and Richard Lacayo, *Law and Disorder*, TIME, April 1, 1991, at 18 (describing recent examples of police abuse of citizens in America, including the well-publicized Los Angeles police beating of Rodney King on March 3, 1991).
11. Mary Ann Williams, *Torture in Chicago*, 12 CHI. LAWYER 1 (No. 3, March 1989) (police manhunt for person who murdered two officers resulted in almost 200 persons mailing complaints about police brutality that occurred within a few hours of the shooting).
12. Michael Kramer, *Gates: The Buck Doesn't Stop Here*, TIME, April 1, 1991, at 25 ("[a] near majority of Los Angeles residents say in a poll they fear for their safety when stopped by an L.A. cop, and a quarter say they have personally seen or have personally been involved in a situation in which excessive force has been used . . .")
13. *See* Kent Greenfield, *Cameras in Teddy Bears: Electronic Visual Surveillance and the Fourth Amendment*, 58 U. CHI. L. REV. 1045, 1046–49 (1991) (describing easily concealed "Electronic Video Surveillance" ("EVS") equipment available on the retail market but used in law enforcement, such as miniature video cameras with pinhole lenses small enough to fit in the palm of a hand and pocket-sized infrared television cameras).
14. Diana Gordon, *Someone to Watch Over Me*, 5 CRIM. JUST. 7 (Spring 1991) (description of use of automated records systems that access federal, state, and local law enforcement data bases that can be used to gather "intelligence" on crime suspects).
15. Special Committee on Criminal Justice in a Free Society, *The Crisis in Our Criminal Justice System*, 4 CRIM. JUST. 18, 37 (No. 4, Winter 1990).

16. Paul Drecksel, *The Crisis in Indigent Criminal Defense*, 44 ARK. L. REV. 363 (1991).

17. *See* Arthur Rosett & Donald Cressey, JUSTICE BY CONSENT: PLEA BARGAINING IN THE AMERICAN COURTHOUSE (1976).

18. *See* Miranda v. Arizona, 384 U.S. 436, 541 n. 5 (1966)(White, J., dissenting) (of 33,381 criminal defendants disposed of in federal cases in 1964, only 12.5 percent of these cases were actually tried). It has been estimated that guilty pleas account for over 90 percent of judgments of conviction. *See* ABA STANDARDS RELATING TO PLEAS OF GUILTY 1–2 (1968).

19. American Bar Association Criminal Justice Section, *Criminal Justice in Crisis* (1988).

20. *Id.* at 4.

21. Samuel Dash & Sharon Goretsky, *We Don't Need to Give Up Our Constitutional Protections to Fight the War on Drugs*, 5 CRIM. JUST. 3 (No. 1, Spring 1990).

22. *Id. at* 54.

23. Dash & Goretsky, *supra* note 21.

24. McClesky v. Zant, 111 S. Ct. 1454 (1991) (prisoner commits "abuse of writ" of habeas corpus by filing successive petition asserting a constitutional claim not raised in his initial petition because of inexcusable neglect or deliberate abandonment).

25. Gregg v. Georgia, 428 U.S. 153 (1976).

26. Delo v. Stokes, 110 S. Ct. 1880 (1990) (district court abused discretion in entertaining new constitutional claim and granting stay of execution in response to petitioner's successive petition, which was an abuse of the writ); Barefoot v. Estelle, 463 U.S. 880 (1983) (a stay of execution pending disposition of successive habeas corpus petition should only be granted where petitioner demonstrates "substantial grounds" for relief).

27. United States v. Salerno, 481 U.S. 739 (1987)(federal Bail Reform Act of 1984 provision that allows pre-trial detention of arrestee on grounds such detention is necessary to the "safety of any other person or the community" is constitutional).

28. McNeil v. Wisconsin, 111 S. Ct. 2204, 2210 (1991).

29. 482 U.S. 496 (1987).

30. 490 U.S. 805 (1989).

31. 482 U.S. at 504; 490 U.S. at 810.

32. 482 U.S. 505–507; 490 U.S. 810–11.

33. *Id.*

34. 111 S. Ct. 2597.

35. *See id.* at 2601–09.

36. *Id.* at 2609–10.

37. *Id.* at 2609.

38. *Id.* at 2610.

39. *Id.*

40. *Id.* at 2610–11.

41. *Id.* at 2619 (Marshall, J., dissenting).

42. *Id.*
43. *Id.* at 2621.
44. *Id.* at 2622.
45. *Id.* at 2623.

Index